T.R.U.E.
FULFILLMENT

HOW TO CREATE LASTING
HAPPINESS IN A WORLD OBSESSED
WITH TEMPORARY PLEASURE

by

JOE ELPHICK

TRUE Fulfillment

How to Create Lasting Happiness in a World Obsessed with
Temporary Pleasure

Paperback ISBN: 978-1-967587-03-2
eBook ISBN: 978-1-967587-04-9

CONTENTS

This book is dedicated to my three daughters, Amy, Joey, and Jessy. All three are unique in their own way, with one thing in common, their golden hearts.

This book was spiritually driven by my younger brother Timmy. The good Lord took him to heaven sooner than later. I just wish he took his cell phone with him!

This book would've never happened if it wasn't for my wife, Lou Ann. Her constant encouragement gave me all the nudges needed not only to begin this book; but also, to arrive at completion. As a nurse practitioner, she has provided strong guard rails for my health.

FOREWORD

FOREWORD BY ROCKY RAUSCH
DOCTORATE IN THEOLOGY

Joe Elphick is my friend, albeit a new friend. His invitation to me to be a sounding board for an idea he had (that eventually became the book you are now reading) was exciting. "Absolutely, Joe I'd love to." I thought to myself what a great way to get to know my new friend even better. His idea of unpacking the Ten Commandments in a way that would be heard by a new generation was intriguing to me. He had a growing uneasiness over the Ten Commandments being barred from some public forums making them less familiar to today's younger generation. I get it. A loving parent and grandparent wants the best for his family. Joe wants them to have every chance to be fulfilled, to be at peace, to thrive and be happy. Joe and I are very aligned in this wish for all families.

For most of my adult life, I have been a student of theological thought. I have been interested in how to effectively present God's love to disillusioned and skeptical people. I believe God's love is real and demonstrated each day in countless ways, and it has been that way throughout history. Why the disconnect then between His unconditional love and human understanding? That's a question that cannot be completely answered in this foreword but a partial explanation is reflected in the words of Jim Rayburn the founder of Young Life. Rayburn's life thesis was that it is simply a crime to bore anyone with and misrepresent the message of God's love. Many misunderstand God because they are never presented with a life-giving, authentic, and personal picture of His love for them.

In *TRUE Fulfillment,* Joe has successfully unpacked the key to living a fulfilled and happy life. That is not to say there isn't life in the original tablets presented to humankind through Moses. As an aside, I believe Moses may have looked a lot like Joe Elphick. However, Joe has now translated these longstanding truths by offering pragmatic practices to flesh out their meaning. His charge is to offer others a living, breathing example of how to love one another. Practicing Joe's principles extends love to others and transforms us in the process.

I live with Joe in a small community in North Carolina. I am witness to Joe living these principles every day. He is a pleasure to know, to watch, to live life with, and to enjoy. His examples in the book are true. He exudes kindness, and it is returned. He is quietly, seemingly effortlessly, and yet effectively, demonstrating how to truly love.

I believe relationships are the cornerstone of our lives. A relationship with God is central to living a fulfilled life, and I believe authentic loving relationships are also a cornerstone. Joe "Mr. Happy" Elphick is helping us all enjoy these relationships. Thank you, Joe.

Dr. Rocky Rausch (D.Min)

INTRODUCTION

THE TEN COMMITMENTS TO TRUE HAPPINESS

Years ago, I attended a week-long public speaking seminar. Not only was I taught how to sharpen my public speaking skills, I was taught how to handle live television interviews and master the art of debate. What I remember most was that the best way to win a debate is to take the opposing side and try to strengthen that position—research the opposing view—then try to improve it! Once I did that, I was truly prepared to contradict those points by researching examples that could influence the weakening of those positions.

At the beginning of the seminar, we were told we would participate in a debate as a conclusion to the week. The topic for the debate would be "Religion, good or bad for mankind?"

After hearing that, I hoped that the instructor would put me on the debating side of "Religion is good for mankind." That would be a no-brainer for me to defend. After all, I was raised with a God-fearing Christian upbringing, memorizing the Q&As of the Baltimore Catechism, and had a mother who excelled in spankings if one of her children deviated from good behavior.

We had all week to think about this debate, and as the week progressed, we realized this debate would illustrate what we had learned that week. Each participant was given one full day to research their positions individually. Then, we were invited to meet our allies on the debate team for four hours to share our different findings. But the stressor was not knowing what position each of us would take until the morning of our library research.

Now, whether you would have argued for or against religion, I bet there is one thing we can all agree on: we all want something good for mankind. We all want a better world. My greatest wish for you is that by the time you finish this book, you will see ways that you can make the world a better place. This book is going to help you be happier, and the things you learn will contribute to not only your own happiness but the happiness of others, too, helping you to make a difference in the world.

Back to the debate. Much to my chagrin, the instructor informed me that I had to debate and support the side that "Religion was *bad* for mankind." My stomach sank; this was not what I had envisioned when I signed up. What an empty feeling I had!

I spent a full day researching religions of the world, from the beginning of AD to the present. I learned a lot about the cruelties of the Crusades. I also learned how many wars had used religion as a catalyst to energize humans to become warriors: Protestants against Catholics in Ireland, the domino theory of communism to fuel the Vietnam War, etc. In the end, I learned a lot—and my team won the debate that "Religion is Bad for Mankind".

As fun as it was to argue and win, doing the research didn't change where I stood: After that, I still truly believed that religion is good for mankind, and my opinion is the same today. I also believe that if you can't find an organized religion that fits your life, you can still focus on leading a life of spirituality, living principles that will both help you and all of mankind.

Through my research, I was able to see how religion had created problems for the human race over time. *Still*, I reasoned, *religion teaches us good things*. The Ten Commandments teach us basic principles for living. But when I asked religious people—like my own daughters, who went to a Christian faith-based school—to recite the Ten Commandments, they couldn't do it. Then, I asked other people, whether they had degrees in theology or were devout Christians, the same question. "Can you recite the Ten Commandments?" And it was amazing to me how many people could not recite them in sequential order.

You don't hear them taught in schools, and even churchgoers don't know them. Yet, the Ten Commandments can teach us to be better. If we understand what they mean in our modern era and we learn what we should do because of them, the world will become a better place.

THE TEN COMMANDMENTS: A STARTING POINT FOR HAPPINESS

In this book, you will hear me talk about each of the Ten Commandments. However, this isn't a religious book. It's not about how to be a better Christian. It's about how to be a better human.

This book is for you if you find yourself searching for happiness, but you're not sure where or how to find it exactly. Whether or not you are religious, you can learn from principles that have helped people find more happiness for centuries.

Because of this, I want to encourage you to read this book with the perspective of a human being, not as someone coming from any particular faith. The Ten Commandments can help us, because we're all a part of the human race. They serve as a moral imperative that forms an ethical foundation.

In my opinion, the Ten Commandments will always be relevant. Maybe they won't be accepted by everyone because they are religious doctrine, but as a collective group, they are still applicable as an outline suitable for modern human behavior. Talking about them as Ten Commandments, though, has become hard for people to understand since it's hard to accept antiquity. The Ten Commandments resonated in ancient times when life was very different, and they don't always land the same way in modern times.

But what if we transitioned the Ten Commandments into *modern commitments*–a list of do's instead of don'ts? Then, we will not only promote positive actions toward our neighbors, but we will also be recipients of the amazing concepts the commitments explore. This is when we will be further encouraged to continue and magnify these positive endeavors.

As I pondered this idea, I realized the Ten Commandments focus on "thou shalt not". That's when I felt the urge to point out the obvious: the Ten Commandments tell you what *not* to do.

This book is going to take a more positive approach to the Ten Commandments. We're going to look at each one and find something we *should* do or *can* do to achieve TRUE happiness (which I'll explain in a moment) based on what we see inside each commandment.

We can all feel happiness in simple moments during the day: an ice cream cone or a nice dinner, for example. But TRUE happiness is more than an event. It's a journey. When you follow the 10 modern, positive commitments that are based on the Ten Commandments, the ones I outline in this book, you will be on a journey to TRUE happiness. Because when you use these concepts in your life, you will become a truly happy person.

TRUE HAPPINESS

Where are you on the voyage to true happiness?

This book is for you if:

1 – You are searching for TRUE happiness but seem unable to find it. The happiness you do find is fleeting, and you feel a pull toward something deeper.

2 – You are just beginning the ride to TRUE happiness. You have started to get glimpses of deeper joy, and you want to build on the momentum you have created. If this is you, then this book will serve as your Google map to get you there.

3 – You are currently enjoying TRUE happiness and want to fine-tune your endeavors, keeping you on your voyage.

No matter how much happiness you are experiencing now, you probably want more. But you may not be sure how to find it. As you read this book, I encourage you to keep an optimistic attitude and believe that you *can* be happier. To take the voyage to TRUE happiness that you are embarking on as you read this book, you have to *believe* that you're going to get there. As you read on, simply believing that there is more TRUE happiness for you will open up your mind to see the growing possibilities for this type of happiness.

Anyone can be happy for a moment. But TRUE, long-lasting happiness is based on lasting principles. The concepts in this book have been studied scientifically and are proven in my own life and the lives of millions of other people around the world.

TRUE Happiness refers to a specific method I am going to use inside these pages. Each of the chapters will use the TRUE method to break down each concept and help you to understand the Ten Commandments from a modern perspective—The 10 Commitments. My goal is to point out how the concepts held in each Commandment can lead to happiness now. Let's take a look at what each letter stands for in the TRUE acronym.

T – Test the traditional view

When looking at the Ten Commandments, we are going to first notice the way that each one was originally intended for an ancient audience. We can see how this perspective has shaped behavior and kept people on a helpful path forward. Most of the Ten Commandments are written as restrictions, or things we should avoid doing. And most of them are things we should definitely avoid if we want happy lives. But there is more that we can do that will lead to TRUE happiness, and that's where the R comes in.

R – Reframe to the positive inverse

We are going to flip each commandment around to see what we need to be actively doing for a happier life, not just those things we need to avoid. In each chapter, I will identify the positive behaviors associated with the inverse of each commandment that brings happiness: what we need to do rather than what we need to not do. Every one of these happiness-building attributes is backed by science that proves how each concept is a stepping stone to a happier life.

U – Understand the deeper purpose

Next comes U, where we study the deeper purpose behind each Commandment and seek to understand why it matters in our lives. We will see that research shows very specific benefits for living the commitments to happiness that I will outline in coming chapters.

E – Embrace the new commitment

Finally, we embrace the new commitment. This is where we put the positive principle into practice. You will immediately notice the effect that living each commitment has on you and others. As you start to make each commitment a habit, your happiness will grow and become a natural part of who you are. In each chapter, I will share examples of how others and I have embraced each commitment and the positive difference it has made in our lives.

So, as we T – test the traditional view, R – Reframe to the positive inverse,

U – Understand the deeper purpose, and E – Embrace the new commitment, we are learning the formula for TRUE Happiness—happiness that is deep and meaningful, the kind that will last a lifetime.

When you find alignment in your life and your relationships with others, following the positive side of each of the Ten Commandments, you will be well-equipped to enjoy the journey toward TRUE Happiness.

In each chapter, I will take you through the commandment and how we can look at it with a positive, modern-day spin. We will focus on what we SHOULD do vs. what we SHOULD NOT do. Each Chapter will start with a **commandment,** then illustrate a positive direction via theory, examples, quotes, etc., and finish with a **commitment** to help you reflect further on the idea and also put it into practice.

I have included 10 Commitments that go with each of the Ten Commandments. But I realize that maybe I have missed one or more commitments to happiness that you have found in your own life. If so, will you share them with me? Feel free to send me an email at truefulfillment@ fastmail.com to tell me what commitments you are living for a happier life.

As you read this book, I suggest you go slowly, reading one chapter a week. Then, spend the rest of each week thinking about how you can make that chapter's concept a part of your life. This will help you ingrain each idea into your mind and into your actions.

TRUE Happiness can be a journey that you begin today. And it will be a journey to cherish, and it is a journey that will have no end!

Chapter 1

FORGIVENESS

"Thou Shalt Not Have Strange Gods Before Me."

In this chapter, the commandment we're reviewing says, "You shall not have strange Gods before me." Different religions have varying opinions on who God is and our relationship with Him, and those differences have caused division through the ages. However, we have only one human race.

So, instead of taking the approach of our relationship to God, I want us to think of this topic in terms of the relationship we have with God's creation–all of mankind. As we relate to the human race, we cannot escape the fact that nobody is perfect, meaning that we will have negative experiences with our fellow imperfect human beings. Some will be on purpose, some will be accidental, and some will just be without explanation.

"Strange Gods" (as stated in the commandment) could be interpreted as those things that can antagonize human relationships. But if we respect each other (as God's collective creation), it will help us to look for ways of forgiving those who might have offended us. How? Through the power of forgiveness, because it is what nurtures human relationships. When we forgive others, we eliminate Strange Gods and see what we have in common with other members of the human race.

Instead of focusing on "thou shalt not", let's talk about "thou shall." When we build as many good human relationships as we can maintain with excellence, this will enrich the quality of our lives. And to take things a step further, our world would be better if we could all find more forgiveness. Forgiveness is that step further to make the world a better place.

Forgiveness is an expression that comes from a position of enormous strength. Whether you are being forgiven or you are the one doing the forgiving, letting go of past wrongs will give you a fresh start. And in order to let go, it requires great strength.

If, from this position of strength, we can acknowledge our own imperfections first, since we're all imperfect, we see that forgiveness is the step that will bring happiness. Forgiveness will help us move through past mistakes and the bad things that have happened to us.

Life is filled with friendships, fights, and misunderstandings. Forgiving is what makes it all better, and what makes us all stronger. And, in fact, this is a vital topic of study around the world.

For example, Dr. Frederic Luskin, Director of The Stanford University Forgiveness Project, developed a program that teaches others to forgive.

He was able to work with women in Northern Ireland whose sons were murdered during the political struggles between Protestants and Catholics (from 1968-1998).

These mothers had to deal with the harsh reality of their sons being shot or beaten based solely on their political or religious beliefs. Because of this, these mothers carried around a great deal of hurt and anger, and they struggled to forgive those who hurt and killed their children.

After the forgiveness training, these women realized they were experiencing noticeable results. They were happier. They were able to let go of the hurt and anger that was weighing them down. And best of all, what they experienced was long-lasting. What they learned in Dr. Luskin's program allowed them to permanently let go and forgive.[1]

Other research has shown that forgiveness reduces stress and improves mental health and self-esteem. Boiled down, this means we feel better about ourselves when we choose to forgive other people.[2]

A MORE PEACEFUL WORLD

Think about it. If everyone forgave each other, we would live in a more peaceful world. Forgiving is a great foundation for happiness, TRUE happiness. Forgiveness gives us closer, more positive relationships instead of distanced, negative relationships. If we think about this in another way, forgiveness also results in fewer enemies. And we could all use fewer of those.

Now, there will always be people out there that you won't want to forgive. If you choose not to forgive them, then you can make a decision to find peace by staying away

1 https://positivepsychology.com/psychology-of-forgiveness/

2 https://www.apa.org/monitor/2017/01/ce-corner

from them as much as possible. Choose carefully who you allow in your life and don't spend time with those who bring unhappiness. Doing so will only cause the feelings associated with unforgiveness to grow bigger inside of you, which will cause your outside actions to become more and more negative. However, when you are able to forgive, you take a roadblock away from yourself, and you no longer need to avoid certain people.

Forgiving helps you embrace a new beginning. It allows you to start all over again without hanging onto any related anger.

A great example of letting go of anger happened several years ago in New York. A woman named Victoria Ruvolo was driving down the highway one night. She didn't know it, but above her on the overpass, a young man named Ryan held a frozen turkey over the unknowing cars passing beneath him. When Victoria's car approached, he let it drop, just for the thrill. The turkey shattered Victoria's windshield and crushed all the bones in her face. During recovery, she heard that the boys who had been with Ryan during the incident agreed to testify against him so the court had enough evidence to put Ryan in jail for 25 years. Victoria said:

> It was at this point that I started asking questions about Ryan. I wanted to know what type of kid would do this.
>
> Had he always been a bully? Was he always hurting other people? What could possibly have built up inside him that was so bad that he had to throw

something so hard? I felt strongly that I didn't want to be responsible for taking this young person's life. I didn't want Ryan to rot in jail.

That's when I asked to meet with Ryan's lawyer to be able to tell him that I wanted an amnesty for Ryan, or at least a lesser sentence.

Because I asked for amnesty for Ryan, he received a six-month prison sentence with five years' probation of community service and psychiatric help. Some people couldn't understand why I'd done this, but I felt God had given me a second chance, and I wanted to pass it on. I know I did the right thing.[3]

Forgiving Ryan when Victoria didn't have to, contributed to her TRUE happiness.

FORGIVENESS DESERVED

Forgiveness is easier to extend to people who are truly sorry for what they've done. After Ryan's incident with the turkey, he felt extreme remorse. Later, a reporter recorded that Victoria and Ryan shared a hug in the courtroom where he sincerely apologized as tears streamed down his face. If someone shows sincere regret for their actions, often, that means they're not going to do the same thing again.

They've repented.

I'll use alcohol as an example. If you are drinking every day, and every time you get drunk, you act badly and you keep saying, "I'm sorry" to your spouse, but then do it again the

---

3   https://www.theforgivenessproject.com/stories-library/victoria-ruvolo/

next day, that's not repenting. When you quit drinking and fix your problem, that's when you've truly repented. You changed your behavior to demonstrate your remorse.

I'm sure you've also heard the saying, "Actions speak louder than words." You can feel when someone is sincere versus just using the words, "I'm sorry," which often feel empty of meaning. Words come out very quickly, but just because someone says they're sorry doesn't mean you have to forgive them, especially if you haven't noticed real repentance.

A NEUTRAL STATE

There will be those times when a person doesn't give you a sincere apology, and instead of refusing that apology, you may then decide to enter into a neutral state. It could be that they aren't someone you are close to, meaning that they don't have the context of who you are to know how they have offended you. In this neutral state, you haven't chosen full-on forgiveness, but you realize that you don't need to go to that level because the relationship isn't an integral part of your world.

Neutrality is where you actively decide you're not going to fight about whatever happened—you're not going to stay mad over the way things happened. You can accept that they're not sorry, choose not to forgive that person, but live in the same world without holding on to anger. You can keep the person at a distance; you don't have to bring them into your close circle. Neutrality is a choice to use for people you don't know that well. In that neutral state, you're being congenial, but you're really not engaging.

Sometimes there are offenses that are bigger and more harmful, but we still haven't heard a sincere apology. For example, maybe the person who has wronged us has died.

When a person dies, you no longer have the hope or possibility that they will apologize. Still, letting go of any related hatred toward them will help you. You can choose the neutral position, which helps you avoid continuing to feel deep, ongoing anger toward that individual.

FORGIVENESS IS A SIGN OF STRENGTH

Forgiveness is something that the strong do best. If another person is truly apologetic, and you don't forgive them, it will help you to ask whether you're not able to forgive them out of personal weakness.

If you want to campaign against this person after they've given you a true apology, you have the option of going in two directions. You're going to work on forgiving or distancing yourself from them. It takes strength to get past whatever happened and to forget the past. But it also takes strength to build boundaries around people who don't value you in order to protect yourself from further hurt by creating that distance.

The amazing thing about forgiveness, though, is that it can change you even when the other person rejects it. Forgiving has the power to change your character. It is beneficial for you no matter what the circumstances are. If someone is truly sorry, and you sincerely forgive them, the wrong action that has worked on your heart begins to go away, and positive things can happen because of that: such as a good friendship instead of hurt feelings and distance, possibly a severing of a relationship.

When you choose not to forgive, you will often feel unhappy because you are stuck carrying a grudge. As you talk about the grudge to yourself and others, it has the potential to grow bigger and bigger and bigger. Instead of fighting a gorilla that is 300 pounds, it has grown to 500 pounds. This can only lead you down a negative path.

On the other hand, it defines your nature if you're a forgiving person. When I write that, I don't mean a person who forgives anybody or everything, but a person who is able to discern when the other party is repentant and then get beyond something horrible that has been done to them.

CHALLENGES OF FORGIVENESS

The challenges of forgiving are internal. Each one of us has to decide if an apology is sincere or insincere and whether it makes sense for us to forgive the other person. You feel better when you forgive, even if someone repeats the same offensive behavior.

If they do it again, learn from that and pause to reevaluate your situation with them. Sometimes, one transgression or offense is enough, depending on who that person is. Is it your daughter? You need to keep working on the relationship. Is it the postman? That's a totally different situation.

It will help to ask yourself if you want to forgive because you really want to be close. The relationship itself matters when you consider how much energy you will need to spend in order to forgive the other person.

There are a lot of things in life you can just let go of. If you get cut off in traffic, you don't know who the driver is. You'll probably never see that person again. This example isn't so much a matter of forgiveness as it is of tolerance and stress management: YOU CAN CHOOSE TO LET IT GO!!!

Yes, he may have almost killed you by driving dangerously. If he's a jerk, he's just one of many out there, but he's not in your circle. So, let the feelings roll off you like water on a duck for that one, because these sorts of things will happen in daily life.

When you experience circumstances like this, it can help you to take a step back.

With stressful situations, we have the option to choose what to do, but it doesn't require the same level of forgiveness. We can choose to take on that stress, or we can ignore that stress. Let it drive away with the car that just cut you off. Why ruin your day over something that really only caused you to hit the brakes? You didn't get in a car accident. No one's hurt, so you are able to choose to get over it without ruining your nice day.

APOLOGIES BUILD RELATIONSHIPS

Forgiveness also comes into play more often when the people involved are closer to you.

In most cases, we want forgiveness to stem from an apology: we realize that the other person is sorry. How do you forgive somebody if you don't know if they're going to do it again and again and again? You aren't inclined to forgive in that situation.

But if an acquaintance says, "The other night I called you a jerk at the party, and I shouldn't have done that. Let's talk about it—let me buy you a drink," that's when you can start all over again. It seems like a true apology, which is probably more genuine since somebody you don't know is going out of his way to apologize to you. When someone makes things right in that way, it accelerates the friendship.

If an acquaintance doesn't apologize, that's when you have your choice to leave that person at a distance and acknowledge that this might not be a person you want to hang around. You probably won't even ask for an apology because who knows if they're sorry. It is helpful to remember, as you think about the concept of forgiveness, that you get to choose your friends and who you want to be close to.

If people are not apologizing, then why forgive them? That's their way of life. This book is about TRUE happiness and how to stay happy by applying what we learn from the Ten Commandments to our modern world. Forgiving doesn't mean you just forgive everybody and every wrong done to you.

Forgiveness can sometimes heal good relationships. When a relationship is worth saving, it is worth going through the effort and being a strong person to forgive.

TRUE APOLOGIES

Forgiveness has to be based on a true apology. The person has to admit they're wrong and promise to commit to trying their best to never to do that again. They can't justify why they are right if they are really sorry.

This actually happened many years ago when I heard a woman say something offensive. Afterward, that woman's apology was, "Well, I'm really sorry I said that to her, and

I shouldn't have said that to her. But, you know what? She got me so angry," and she started justifying why she did something wrong instead of leaning into her simple apology.

When a person is giving a true apology, they won't justify how what they did was right. Instead, they will admit to wrongdoing and stop there so that the person hearing the apology will see their remorsefulness. The feeling behind it matters as much or even more than the words being said.

It always becomes easier to forgive somebody if you can see that they are sincerely sorry.

USING COMPASSION TO UNDERSTAND OTHERS

When someone you love is in a bad place and they do something wrong, you can choose to forgive them because, even though they may do it again, you understand that they're not capable of changing at that moment.

When you have the context of who a person is, you can choose to give them both compassion and grace, even if they're not able to apologize or able to fully change in that moment. Raising kids is a perfect example.

One of my three daughters would let a bad day at school make our family evenings at home challenging.

I remember once coming home from work, and my daughter and my wife were yelling and screaming at each other. My wife said that our daughter had been driving her crazy all day, using bad language, and being disrespectful. I calmly told my daughter to go outside, cool off, and I would meet her in the gazebo to deal with whatever was wrong.

The two of us initially sat there in silence for just a few minutes, but it felt like hours. I broke the silence by stating,

"We're not leaving here until we get to the bottom of this."
Still, we sat with both our sets of eyes looking at the floor, silent.

Then, all of a sudden, she started complaining about her mother, her day, and everything that had gone wrong. I just listened, not saying a word, just looking her in the eye. And finally, she broke down with this huge scream and cried out that some boy in her school called her fat in the morning, and that was the real issue—it was nothing that her mother had done!

I said, "Stand up. Give me a hug." She gave me a big hug. She cried her eyes out and I held her tightly.

I said, "You should apologize to your mom." We went inside and told her mom what had happened that day. My daughter sincerely apologized to her mother who immediately forgave her and gave her a big hug, saying, "Oh, my God, I am so sorry. I didn't realize you were hurting. Thank you for apologizing, and of course, you're forgiven!"

The deeper the relationship is to you, the more you're willing to listen so you can understand, and that understanding opens you up to forgiveness.

With our daughter, all the anger just melted away because we came to understand what was going on with her. We knew she was hurting, but we also knew she would eventually rise above that and move on. And that she did!

THE SECRET KEY: WHY FORGIVENESS MAKES ALL THE DIFFERENCE

Forgiveness comes from a sense of strength. The strong forgive, while the weak cannot or will not. It only makes sense that a strong, forgiving person is much happier than someone who is unforgiving and carries grudges. When you forgive somebody, you can do more than just accept their apology, you can explain why you're forgiving them. When you explain the WHY behind your forgiveness, that truly connects you to that person on a deeper level.

True forgiveness has the same effect as a true apology. Think of it as an equation. If somebody takes the time to offer a true apology, you should offer that person the same energy back in terms of forgiveness and let them know that the apology meant something to you. You can share with them that it felt really great to hear from them. You could reimburse them with the same level of forgiveness in relation to their apology to make them feel great.

When you master true forgiveness in your relationships, you have another building block in your foundation of TRUE happiness.

Let me give you an example of what I mean. Have you ever gone to a restaurant and had the waitress take your order, only to have something other than what you ordered show up? On the other hand, have you ever gone to a restaurant and the waitress takes your order, and then she repeats back to you what you ordered? When the food came out, in that case, it was probably just how you wanted it.

This is a great example of how clear communication works. You have an open line of connection and you both know exactly what was said. It was reinforced. So when somebody apologizes to you, if you do that same thing and read back to them their apology and how you feel about it, you're validating it as a true apology and offering your true forgiveness.

Each person is happier that the bad act, whether you gave it or received it, is behind you all. It will help if you take the time to communicate this true forgiveness in a setting where that person cannot only hear your forgiveness but also see the forgiveness in your eyes. Then, try to finish your true forgiveness with a handshake or a hug.

SINCERITY MATTERS

When talking about forgiveness, sincerity has to be the primary ingredient. Real repentance can't be a facade. It's got to be heartfelt. It's got to be serious.

When someone is serious enough to apologize, you have to match that same emotional energy to show that sincerity exists on both ends. We'll think better of the person giving the apology and we'll think better of the person doing the forgiving if there's sincerity and eye contact.

The one thing that will break each and every relationship you have is continuing to only think of yourself. If you're truly sincere in forgiving, you're thinking of that other person. When you see what they're feeling, you're feeling it too, and you are able to let go of your own pain.

FORGIVENESS IN DAILY LIFE

Let the goal be forgiveness. Learn to forgive whatever problems you have. Figure out ways to forgive or be forgiven, whatever the stressor is, in any relationship you have.

Here are some questions to ask yourself. You can also ask the other person for their feedback:

What did I do to offend that person, or what did they do that made me feel offended? What could I have done differently? Did I do something wrong? Did I provoke the other person?

These questions will help you get more curious about the situation so that you can see things in a different light. Go through that process with the other person and take the time to self-inspect.

THREE SECRET KEYS TO FORGIVENESS IN DAILY LIFE

- **Step one:** Avoid revenge. Two wrongs never make a right! And if you do wrong to another person, you then owe them a true apology and that complicates things further.
- **Step two:** Be prudent! Stay aware of people who cannot be trusted with outward forgiveness. Keep them in a more neutral relationship instead of letting them into your close circle.
- **Step three:** Realize that in the end, delivering true forgiveness will bolster your TRUE happiness.

REFLECTION POINTS

Think about an event in your life that required you to forgive (perhaps something you are still upset about) as you answer the following questions.

- Did the person express genuine remorse for their actions?
- Based on your reflections, do you think this was a "true apology"? Why or why not?

- If you choose to forgive this person, what will change? How will you feel afterward?
- Do you believe this person is truly sorry and has shown efforts to change?
- Can you let go of the hurt, even if you don't forget the action?
- What might you need to feel fully ready to forgive?
- If you can't forgive this person yet, how can you still move forward without letting this offense control your emotions?
- What can you do to maintain emotional distance without allowing negativity to consume you? How can you move forward peacefully?

The person who benefits the most from forgiveness is not the one being forgiven, it is the one doing the forgiving. From forgiving others, you will start to see the world differently.

At some point in your life, you will also make mistakes. In fact, you might offend someone intentionally or unintentionally. But through being a true forgiveness practitioner, you will comprehend how to deliver a meaningful "true apology" versus a "casual apology."

The commandment to have "no strange gods before me" teaches us in our modern world about the commitment to forgive. We exercise strength of character every time we forgive someone who has wronged us. But forgiving also frees us from carrying around the burden of hurt and anger.

The 1st Commitment to TRUE Happiness is: Choose to show your strength by forgiving others.

"To forgive is to set a prisoner free; and discover the prisoner was you."

—Lewis B. Smedes

Chapter 2

KINDNESS

"Thou Shalt Not Take the Name of the Lord Thy God in Vain."

Like many of the Ten Commandments, this commandment is telling us NOT to do something, rather than encouraging us to do something. As we talk about the second commandment, we will expand the idea of how we talk about the Lord with respect to how we talk about everyone around us. Rather than targeting other members of the human race with curses or gossiping, do the opposite: express kindness to your fellow human beings.

Kindness goes beyond just our words. It includes our actions and how we treat others, which encompasses everything from generous actions and nurturing words to active listening.

An interesting study was done in Japan. Researchers asked a group of college students to count the kind acts they performed over the course of a week. They were to note every time they were kind and record how they felt.

As you would expect, people who did more kind acts were happier. But the study uncovered another interesting fact: people who *paid more attention* to the kind acts they did were also happier. Just noticing kindness increases our joy![4] When we make an effort to be kind and spend time thinking of nice things to do for others, we will find more TRUE happiness in our lives.

Other studies show that the happiness we feel from being kind can actually change our brain, giving us more of the brain chemicals we need to feel good.[5]

It's easier for me to spend time thinking about being kind when I am with kind people. One way I focus on kindness is when I witness other people performing random acts of kindness. If I see someone pay for a stranger's coffee or hold open a door for the next person walking in, it inspires me to do similar acts of kindness. When I do, I notice that I have an increased sense of well-being.

LIVING WITH KINDNESS

If we all lived with more kindness toward those around us, we would all experience the same sense of well-being that I have. It's easier to pay attention to the unkind things others do than to highlight the good. The truth is, we all make mistakes. Like we talked about in Chapter 1, we will be a lot happier if we forgive and let some of that go. If we instead choose to focus on the good that others are doing, and increase the ways we are kind, all of this positive energy could only lead to increased TRUE happiness.

This kindness can even come in the business world. In

---

4 https://pmc.ncbi.nlm.nih.gov/articles/PMC1820947/

5 https://unlimitedloveinstitute.org/downloads/ITS-GOOD-TO-BE-GOOD-2014-Biennial-Scientific-Report-On-Health-Happiness-Longevity-And-Helping-Others.pdf

my career, our company had an excellent reputation because we were focused on employment retention and the success of our customers. I had some competitors across the United States. We were friends and helped each other. If somebody needed raw materials, and I had sufficient inventory, I would not hesitate to help them. As friendly competitors, we would share innovations, new technologies, safety, best practices, etc. Our mutual kindness yielded mutual successes.

Unfortunately, in 2005, my plant burned to the ground and all of a sudden 80 people were out of work, with no idea when–or if–they would ever return to work again. It seemed like a tragedy at first, but the amount of good that came out of that loss was phenomenal. In my time of need, I had friendly competitors from all over the United States take over my customers' purchase orders. They did the work and sent me an invoice; then, when the goods were delivered to my customers, I invoiced them. Because of my competitors' help, in just nine months, the plant was rebuilt, and I did not lose a single client. Despite what could have been a setback, over the next 15 years, my company was a market leader that grew to nearly 300 employees. There is no way we would have gotten back on our feet without the kindness of the other business owners. I like to think we paved the way for their kindness with our mutual respect and kindness before we were in need.

KINDNESS IS OFTEN RECIPROCATED

It's nice to know that when you make an effort to be kind, you are doing something that can spread. As you can see in the business example above, kindness breeds kindness!

Another example has to do with my passion for offshore competitive fishing. The average cost of a fishing trip to the Gulf Stream is substantial, but I don't ask those who attend these trips to pay. However, even though I ask for nothing in return, the reciprocal, unsolicited kindness often comes back to me and in many forms. People want to do something to show me their appreciation, and they often do this with invites and kind gestures.

When we do something from a motive of true kindness, it will bring TRUE happiness. An important nuance of being truly kind means that you want to help out of a desire for friendship and service, not for what the other person might do for you in exchange. You can't be kind just because you want something in return. When you're truly kind, and you give something away out of kindness, that same kindness can come back to you in various ways, often just by making you feel happier!

I love to cook and invite people to my house. We have a dinner table with 18 seats, and we love to fill it up. Because of our invitations to others, we are often invited to similar events at other people's homes…that's reciprocity at its best.

When people are truly kind, they don't expect reciprocation, but the truth is it often comes flying back. While I was away traveling in Maine two weeks ago, we were hit with a cyclone here on Bald Head Island. The rainwater flooded the garage and area in front of the house, which would have caused major damage if left unattended. While I was gone, my friend Kenny organized everything, pumped the water out, moved my golf carts and took care of all the damage. I had no idea he was going to do that. I think that's where the kindness and generosity came back. A good friendship came from good interactions, dinners at the house, and things of that nature.

I didn't ask for Kenny's kindness. It just happened while I was gone. This comes because I have surrounded myself with kind people who want to do good things. It comes because kind people want to help when they see something go wrong.

CHALLENGES WITH BEING KIND

We all face challenges with being kind sometimes. It's easy to want to focus on yourself or to be concerned about what you'll get and not what you'll give.

And when you read the news, sometimes it's easy to think that no one is kind anymore! Imagine the change if our media somehow started focusing on man's humanity to man versus man's inhumanity to man. That would certainly help bolster global kindness.

But since we might not be able to change the media, we can work to rise above it. We may not be big enough to compete with the media, but we do have the option of changing channels; there are many options we all have to shower each other with good thoughts and to share good things that are happening.

BE KIND FOR THE RIGHT REASONS

One thing is vitally important: You have to be certain that there is nothing expected in return for your good deed. You have to do it for all the right reasons. You want nothing returned. You don't have to make it known to anybody but yourself.

Just stay the course of being kind to people, and yes, there'll be naysayers out there–that's going to happen. But the more you continue to be kind, the more people believe that this is where your soul is, that this is the kind of person you are.

Sometimes when people are negative, they perceive others as negative. A perfect example happened a few months ago. My good friend Tracy donated a substantial amount of money to my charity, The Children's Flight of Hope. A person who heard about it thought his donation was just him showing off. That was a horrible thing for my friend to hear about a beautiful thing that

he had done. But my friend was able to recognize this was just people using negativity as a defense mechanism. This is where good deeds can get punished as the saying goes. But when you focus on kindness, you have to stay the course even when there are naysayers out there.

When others aren't kind to you, just stay strong. You've got to ignore the shallow gossiping that might occur and stay committed for the long haul to be a kind person. If you want TRUE happiness, be that person that is going to be kind the rest of your life—in spite of the naysayers and gossipers.

Just continue the way you are and good things will happen again. When you stay strong and continue your acts of kindness, it doesn't matter what other people say. Your actions will speak louder than words.

KINDNESS SPREADS

Someone whose kind and selfless actions have had a great

impact is Mother Teresa who lived a life of being kind to everybody. She was a very happy woman who had nothing, but her happiness came from helping others and being kind to people. She worked with lepers and the sick. She would take the bread out of her mouth to feed a starving person. Helping people that needed outside assistance brought joy and purpose to Mother Teresa. And through her work, many people were inspired to help others, too. That's how kindness spreads.

Everybody has a different amount in their fuel tank of kindness, depending on upbringing, where they came from, and where they are in their life. And at times, that amount can vary. When people are going through hard times, they can struggle to be kind because of their current situation. But kindness is contagious, so be kind to them anyway.

Kindness really does spread.

SECRET KEY TO KINDNESS IN DAILY LIFE

The biggest key to having more kindness each day is to have quiet time when you wake up in the morning. During your quiet time, think of your scheduled day.

What is ahead of you? Are there meetings? Things you're looking forward to? Things you're dreading? Think of how you could spread kindness in each event.

Put a positive spin on things as much as you can. We all know that human beings are not perfect. But when you look on the bright side and find the good in people (even though you may have to look really hard for the good in some people), that will have a positive impact.

Picture all of your kindness, all of your good deeds, all

your positive attitudes as deposits in a bank account. The more you put in that kindness account, the more you're going to get in return. And I don't mean that you'll get paid back in kindness, but that you'll feel good, you'll have a good attitude, and it'll transform you into a happier person.

Kindness is a great foundation for TRUE happiness.

If you're a parent, you will understand what I mean, but I think nothing is more rewarding for me than being with my three daughters and hearing them tell me about things that other people have said about me—and they're smiling, because they heard their dad was kind. That's what I mean by what you get back–when somebody you love, like your children or grandchildren look up to you, you can know that your kindness impacted them.

REFLECTION POINTS

Because kindness spreads kindness, this exercise will help you remember kind things others have done for you and help you to spread more kindness by acknowledging what others have done.

- Write down the following:
  - » 1- A list of kind acts that have been done for you by members of your family
  - » 2- A list of kind acts that have been done for you by your friends
- Using your list, reach out to each of these people, in person if possible. Acknowledge their kindness and even share with them the examples you thought of.

We started this chapter by talking about the commandment not to "take the name of the Lord in vain." We have discussed how we can instead be kind in our words and our actions. The commitment to kindness changes who we are. The more we look for kindness, the more we see kindness all around us.

The 2nd Commitment to TRUE Happiness is: Nurture human relationships with both kind words and kind actions, expecting nothing in return.

"Whatever possessions we gain by the sword, cannot be sure of lasting...but the love gained by kindness and moderation is certain and durable."

—Alexander the Great

Chapter 3

GRATITUDE

"Remember to Keep Holy the Lord's Day."

The third commandment says to keep the Lord's day holy. When we honor the Lord's day we're being thankful to God for his creation of this earth. We can extend that same gratitude to the whole human race. We can be thankful for other people in our lives, for the relationships we have with them, and for our interactions with the human race. Everything we have is always dependent on others around us.

Multiple studies show that being grateful makes you happier. The correlation has been shown in study after study after study. Grateful people recognize the role that others play in contributing to their happiness.[6] The research also shows that happier people are more grateful.[7] They are able to recognize life's simple pleasures and find gratitude for the small things.[8]

For people who want to be happier, the science is clear:

---

6   https://pmc.ncbi.nlm.nih.gov/articles/PMC1820947/

7   https://guilfordjournals.com/doi/abs/10.1521/jscp.23.5.603.50748

8   https://pmc.ncbi.nlm.nih.gov/articles/PMC1820947/

becoming more aware of the things we are grateful for will increase our happiness. Researchers have long known that people waiting to start therapy are often frustrated by the time it takes to be scheduled for an appointment. To counteract these feelings, researchers suggested those waiting for their first therapy session start a gratitude intervention. In the weeks leading up to therapy, and before they ever met with a therapist, those who focused on gratitude were able to improve their feelings of happiness and well-being.[9]

We can always find things to be grateful for. I want to share this powerful example. I have a friend named Michael who was raised in a violent home and kicked out when he was just a teenager. Living on his own, he found food and shelter where he could, sometimes staying in abandoned cars or sleeping on friends' couches.

Michael tried to put on a brave face, not letting on how alone he really was. But his friend Albert Flood and Albert's parents could see that he needed help. They invited him for dinner one night, and because it was raining, they encouraged him to stay in their guest room. One night turned into two, and two into three, and eventually this became his home. The Floods did more than give Michael food and shelter; they gave him a family.

Michael says about this time, "In the years to follow I learned what life was supposed to be about. My past lessons

---

9 https://www.researchgate.net/publication/262725937_Can_Grati-tude_and_Kindness_Interventions_Enhance_Well-being_in_a_Clini-cal_Sample?__cf_chl_tk=IyUIeiafS.M7X0AhPqynfhEJ1WJLrzvAnfhS8. pCHVA-1737584266-1.0.1.1-nei63lpYwKbwZFmumgvaZE7Yvrvk3Em-quMgRCvnY2e

from my biological family were slowly fading away as the lessons of generosity and gratitude were taking a strong hold. Helping others and being thankful for what I have each day is something that continually grows inside of me each day." The Flood family's kindness helped Michael find the belonging he had been searching for. And the gratitude he felt then has led to his generous nature.

Now, many years later, Michael continues to express his gratitude. He is the first person on Bald Head Island to help others when it's needed, and he is widely considered the most generous person on the island. His gratitude for all the good that comes his way makes him a happy person.

I have also seen gratitude in action when I met Miguel, who was doing some work on our kitchen. Through our kitchen remodeling process, I spent a lot of time getting to know him better. He struck me as a very happy person. He told me that when he was young, he had made some mistakes and ended up spending time in prison. Instead of being bitter, he actually told me it changed his life for the better. It caused him to think about his choices and turn to God. He ended up becoming a chaplain and now personally orchestrates missions to his home country of Puerto Rico, helping the poor and those addicted to drugs. In the short time I knew him, he expressed gratitude for his time in prison, his wife, his job, his health, and more. His favorite saying is, "How blessed am I."

A solid foundation for happiness is to always look for the good things in your life and be thankful for them, like Miguel does. Even challenging things, like spending time in prison, can give us something to be grateful for.

A MATTER OF FOCUS

I'm not telling you to be grateful for bad things. I'm really talking about the idea of what we focus on. Think about trying to listen to the radio. If you are listening to the radio and your favorite song is coming in under static, you can focus on the song or you can focus on the static.

In life, bad things will happen. Just like static happens.

But on any given day you have a choice. You could wake up in the morning, spend two hours saying how miserable the day is going to be, or you could take an hour and say, this is going to be a great day, and this is how I'm going to make it good. I choose not to focus on the bad. I'll let it go. I won't sweat the little things. I will look for ways to be grateful.

I'll never forget the time I was traveling in New York City with a salesman and he left his cell phone in the cab. I said, "You'll never get it back," and he answered, "Well, let's call it up anyway," because he knew he had to get his phone.

He calls his phone, and the cab driver answers it, and says, "Well, meet me on the corner of 42nd and 5th in 35 minutes, and I'll be there." We were both as thankful as could be. It was almost unbelievable to me. The cab drove up, and said, "Here's your phone." The salesman gave the driver 20 bucks and the cab driver said, "I don't make money by doing good deeds. Keep your money. I'm just glad I found your phone for you."

The salesman was grateful, I was grateful, and even the cab driver in that hectic and busy city of New York was grateful that he was able to do something good. That could have been a bad moment, but instead we focused on being grateful.

CHALLENGE: FOCUS ON THE GOOD

As a business owner, I have really tried to help my employees. When I was running my company, I made a point to do good things for them. My goal was to make them feel like owners and give them the chance to obtain the wealth they helped create. We put together an employee stock ownership plan (ESOP) and had a breakfast meeting every quarter.

At that meeting, I'd buy them all breakfast. I was trying to open up the books and let everybody know all about the company as well. I wanted them all to know more about business.

At one of those breakfast meetings, I had one employee that said two things that showed me he didn't understand what we were trying to do as a company (and he wasn't feeling grateful, either.) He said, "Joe, if I own this company, how come we didn't get menus? You just serve this egg pie and I don't like it." Now we were at a nice little restaurant down south that serves these beautiful quiches, or what he called "egg pies."

He went on to say, "I don't know about this ownership. You guys went out and bought a half a million dollar printing press and no one asked me, no one got me involved whatsoever."

I replied to him, "Thank you, good point, I should have asked you if you like egg pie, next time at breakfast we're going to maybe get a little survey. Going back to the part where we bought the printing press, what do you do for this company?"

And he said, "I drive the truck."

"Okay," I said, "how would you feel if we bought a new truck and didn't get you involved?"

"I'd be mad," he answered.

"Of course you would. Do you know when we bought this printing press, we had all the printing managers and all the printing press men involved in this process?"

"No, I didn't know that. So are you saying when you buy a truck, you'll get me involved?"

I said, "Yes, I will."

He goes, "Okay then, thank you." He was very happy. Even though he didn't feel grateful at first, he started to realize all that he had to be grateful for.

He had never been given ownership before. But having ownership gave a lot of wealth to the employees. Because of the clarifications I made in what he did have ownership in, he also saw that I really was interested in having the team members give leadership input on what changes to make. When he understood that, it started to change how he felt.

But he didn't feel grateful until he understood at a deeper level, which helped him change what he was focusing on in order to have gratitude.

TAKE TIME TO BE GRATEFUL

Everybody has the capacity for gratitude in them. We just need to increase our focus on being grateful. Everybody can spend some time, maybe a couple hours a week, to really sit back and look at their lives and be very thankful for all they have. As human beings, we have so much more to be thankful for that we can even think of—if we just made the time to reflect. There are things to be grateful for; we just need to get better at noticing them.

On Sunday, when I go to our small chapel on Bald Head Island, I spend an entire hour just thinking of my whole life, how lucky I am. In spite of a few bad things sometimes happening, I can sit and focus on all the good things in my life. You could find your own quiet place to do the same. Sit in a church or take a walk outside but spend the time thinking of the good in your life and being grateful.

It's hard for me to believe that there are people in this world who have nothing. Even in areas of the world where there is so much political unrest and fighting, people still find things to be grateful for. They can be grateful for their family, their home, for human interaction, for food and sunshine. When there is a negative shadow from all that's going on in their country, they can choose to focus on that and be very unhappy. Or they can focus on what they have, which might outweigh some of the things that sadden them—through gratitude.

We don't usually think: I'm thankful for shoes on my feet, or for the food in my tummy because we often take so many small things for granted. When we don't notice what we have, the value is diminished. But if we're thankful for each of these things, they become valuable.

My wife shared this example with me. She is a nurse practitioner that owns and operates the clinic in Bald Head Island. She gives away a lot of things like band-aids, lotions, and even her time in giving diagnoses. We started to realize that because people were getting stuff for free, they didn't value it and at times, took advantage. But if we instead were to give them a 50 percent discount, they might realize the value and be thankful because they understood the true cost. It can help all of us be more grateful when we understand the value of what we're getting, whether that is an actual monetary cost, or even the value of someone's time.

THE SECRET KEY TO GRATITUDE

Having gratitude is a discipline. Take a Sunday dinner, for example. Let's say you're being served roast beef, brown gravy, corn, broccoli, and mashed potatoes. And if you don't like broccoli, what are you going to choose to think about that meal?

Because you don't like broccoli, is this meal terrible? Or can you choose to look at all the other good food on your plate, and be thankful for everything you have? You don't have to eat the broccoli, but you can make the choice to be thankful for the meal in front of you. It's a discipline to look at all you have versus all that you don't have. Being grateful is a choice.

The secret is to increase your discipline to recognize all the good things in your life and the possibility to add more. Your life is good at this moment, but you also have an ability to make it even greater right now by being more thankful. This is true when you think of setting and achieving goals. You can be grateful for your steps that bring you closer to attaining your goal, or you can focus on the one small misstep or failure you had last week. Don't focus on the one failure you had last week. Focus instead on tomorrow and all the ways you can turn things around. And be grateful for the opportunity to make that change.

NOT AS GRATEFUL AS WE COULD BE

If you show a lack of discipline to take time to review, ponder, and recognize all the good things in your life, this will keep you from feeling gratitude.

If you only focus on things that have gone wrong or the impossibilities of how to move forward, you won't feel grateful. Instead, focus on what is possible, what you can do, and what you will do and have the discipline to think in those terms. When you do, your gratitude will follow naturally.

Once a year on Thanksgiving most people take quiet time to ask themselves what they are thankful for. But we can have Thanksgiving every week! Think about what you're thankful for daily or weekly, not just one day out of the year.

When you think about what you're grateful for, it turns into a huge laundry list of all the good things that are going on in your life. Recognizing all the amazing things in your life will bring you happiness.

It's just like a multi-lane highway. Sometimes people only think in one lane, for example, their health. If they have health issues, they may say, "Oh my god, I've got a doctor appointment this week," or "The pharmacy is expensive," or "It took so long at the doctor's office," and they're stuck in one lane (bad health). But if you show them there are other lanes on the highway, they will realize all there is to be grateful for.

To ease them out of that one lane, you can say, "Oh,

how's your granddaughter doing?" and they might respond, "Oh, she's doing great." You might bring up something that you know they have going for them like, "I bet your pension is still coming." And they might say, "Oh yeah. That was a great job I had." When you have conversations with someone, you have the opportunity to coach them to see all the good instead of the bad lane they're stuck in, like the example of a struggle with bad health. If they get on this one lane highway and stay in that lane, it's hard for them to feel any gratitude. So, we can help others expand to a multi-lane highway of gratitude.

This is also true for ourselves.

GRATITUDE IN DAILY LIFE

Develop the discipline to take quiet time to look at the balance sheet in your life: your challenges on one side and the many good things on the other. Look at all the aspects of your life, not just the bad ones. During my quiet time I always think about my kids, my grandkids, my wife, all the people I love. And then there's always something that has happened that causes me to reflect. I learned recently that a buddy of mine has cancer. I took a moment to look at my own health, and I feel good and strong. It makes me count my blessings for my health while my poor buddy is going through the extreme challenges of chemo. Thinking about my health makes me feel grateful for what I have…and then I want to reach out to my friend with kindness and help him during his challenges.

During that quiet time of reflection about what you have to be grateful for, be mindful of what flows into your head.

For me, I try to actively recognize the gratitude I feel. My chapel here is a great place where I like to be still. It is a quiet time to sit and think about my life once a week and find gratitude.

Use quiet time for self introspection. You may think of a family member you are struggling to get along with. Just pray someday that the situation will get better. Or something terrible may come to mind, like while I was writing this chapter, somebody I knew was hit by a car. But I practiced gratitude when I chose to be grateful for the outcome, "I'm so thankful he didn't get killed." There are so many dimensions of thankfulness. If you ask yourself once a week, "What do I have to be thankful for?" Then reflect on the answer during a quiet time, you'll see how long that list can get.

REFLECTION POINTS

- Schedule one hour a week to reflect on all you are thankful for. Find a place where you can really ponder, like a church or out in nature.

- As you reflect, what comes to mind? Is it material possessions? Relationships? What are you most grateful for?

Committing to **gratitude** means that we choose to look on the bright side. We can always find the good in any situation. When we do this, it makes everything in life happier.

The 3rd Commitment to TRUE Happiness is: Take quiet time to recognize what you have to be thankful for.

"I am happy because I am grateful. That gratitude allows me to be happy."

—*Will Arnett*

Chapter 4

FAMILY

"Honor Thy Father and Mother."

In this chapter, the commandment to honor your father and mother naturally leads us to talking about family. The most basic unit of our society is the family. The mother and father assume a leadership position and a vision for the future of the family.

That being said, we can't control what kind of parents we have, but we can live our lives to be good parents, whether we currently have children or not, and that will lead to TRUE happiness. In this chapter we will focus on family relationships and *being* the kind of parents that deserve honor and respect. Parents have an important role in making the family strong. This happens when they show respect for each other (we'll talk more about respect in Chapter 9).

If you don't have good parents, it's even more of a reason to seek out the right way to live and let your life be an example to your children. You don't get to choose the way you were raised, but you can choose how to raise your own family. Be the parents that you would have wanted to have. Be the kind of person who deserves honor and respect, even if that hasn't been modeled for you by your own parents.

Research has shown that better family relationships can increase well-being, so investing time in your family will pay off in both their happiness and your own.[10] Another consideration linked to happiness is a sense of belonging.[11] As parents, we can work to create a family unit where each family member feels like they are an important part of the family, knowing they belong, no matter what.

Studies also show that what happens in the home and family directly affects how children feel, even more than their school, friends, or community.[12] Building strong family relationships is a commitment to the happiness of the whole family.

For me, family is the largest contributor to my own TRUE happiness. To be loved by my wife, honored by my daughters, and respected by my grandchildren, truly gives me a great sense of well-being.

My daughters know that they belong in a family even with my ex-wife and me. We make a conscious effort to reach out and communicate with each other and make efforts to come together on a regular basis. So much so that we all look forward to it when someone in the family has a birthday because our tradition is to get together for dinner, where we spend time laughing, reminiscing, and telling stories. But belonging in a family is more than just fun

---

10   https://www.sciencedirect.com/science/article/abs/pii/S2212657017301204

11   https://www.journalofhappinessandhealth.com/index.php/johah/article/view/43

12   https://pmc.ncbi.nlm.nih.gov/articles/PMC9778774/#:~:text=In%20particular%2C%20research%20has%20found,%2C%20or%20community%20%5B29%5D

birthday dinners. In my upbringing, my sense of belonging didn't come only from the fun times we had together, but from the chores my parents gave us to do, which gave us pride in our home and family.

When it comes to my relationship with my wife, Lou Ann, we have both been married before. When we made the decision to marry, the major foundation of the mutual attraction we share is the love we have for all of our children who were born of our prior marriages.

Combined we have seven children and eight grandchildren, and maybe more to come. In the early days of our dating, I felt assured that our love of family would serve as the nourishment that would sustain a happy, lifelong relationship. We have been blessed by having two homes, one on the coast and one in the mountains of North Carolina. These two homes are very different in style and elevation; but they have one major feature in common. We have one wall in each home that we collectively call "Our Trophy Walls"—they are walls in our homes that are adorned with many, many framed pictures of ordinary moments in the lives of our extraordinary kids and grandkids.

COMMITMENT TO FAMILY

As a parent, you may wonder if you're doing a good job. The truth is, commitment to your family is what makes you a good parent who deserves honor and respect. Whether you are in a child's life through biology or marriage, you can choose to commit to being there for the child.

In many instances, stepparents have had wonderful impacts on families. I remember hearing about a young bride who was very troubled over the decision of who should walk her down the aisle: her biological father, who had no contact with her over the years, or her stepdad who came into her life at a young age. Her stepdad taught her sports, helped with her homework, and eventually paid for her college education. They had a wonderful, mutually respectful relationship. Her decision really boiled down to thinking about who her biological dad was as a person (and his lack of involvement in her life) and who her stepdad was. The ceremony belonged to the stepfather who was there for her day-to-day life. He had earned the honor of walking her down the aisle; he had earned her respect.

Our good friends Lisa and Alan live a committed life to their family of two adopted daughters. Even though their precious daughters are unrelated in terms of DNA, they represent the true definition of sisters! Both girls are grounded and balanced in their daily lives and have grown up to become responsible wives and mothers because of the role model they had in their own parents. Lisa and Alan, from my perspective, certainly deserve the TRUE Happiness lifetime achievement award!

My parents showed this same kind of commitment to my own family. My mother was very religious. My dad had a sixth grade education and worked two and sometimes three jobs to support ten children. Money was often tight. There were a lot of things we didn't have, but we had a good family structure. Every Sunday, we all got in the station wagon and went to church, listening to services that were said in Latin in the olden days. My parents were very different from each other but they worked together to provide a good spiritual, or religious, framework and they taught us right versus wrong. This proved more important than the amount of money we had in the bank.

Families today also need to be aware of being content and not worrying too much about all the things they don't have. It's so easy to get caught up in the things that don't really matter, always wanting the next thing and focusing on material gains. Instead, focus on nonmaterial gains, like the relationships you have in your family with your parents, your brothers, your sisters, and your friends.

My parents were committed to me and my brothers and sisters. When parents commit to children, it brings the entire family TRUE happiness and earns respect and honor for the parents. Commitment helps each person feel loved and cared for. It gives the parents purpose and meaning. When children are secure in their families, it affects not only them, but others around them.

RIPPLE EFFECTS OF FAMILY RELATIONSHIPS

Because the family unit is the most basic unit of society, if the family is strong, there is a ripple effect. When we have happier families, we have happier neighborhoods. Happier neighborhoods lead to stronger communities. And that comes from committed people trying to be good parents.

What you do in your own family will have an impact on the TRUE happiness of the world around you. But our families don't exist in a vacuum. There are many outside influences that impact them.

CHALLENGES IN MODERN FAMILIES

Families today face many challenges. Some of these stem from elements in our modern society, like social media and comparison with others who have more than us. The structure of the family is changing, with fewer traditional two-parent families than ever before. Many times, our busy lives also make it hard to find the time to prioritize being the kind of parents we want to be.

One of the biggest things parents have to deal with today is the intensifying influence of social media.

Social media seems to be limitless in the good it can offer. Unfortunately though, there is also limitless evil that can be found there. So, to earn their children's respect, parents must remain vigilant and provide guardrails against pervasive negative influences from social media platforms for themselves as well as their children. Every negative aspect in this world can be found and amplified on social media like negative news, fighting, shootings, or other things that weigh heavily on us and can hold significant influence on our lives. When parents protect their children from these negative influences, which their kids might not always appreciate, children will ultimately come to see that their parents are committed to their well-being.

Another challenge that cannot be avoided is how family structures have changed. We have divorce, single parents, kids living with their parent's partner. No matter what the family looks like, the value in those relationships comes from *time* spent in those relationships. It's about quantity, not quality. Good parents commit to spending a lot of time with their kids, even when they don't have any big event scheduled as a family.

Parents can be there, available for whatever comes in the day. Be there for the report card. Be there for their daughter when she wakes up in the morning, help their son brush his teeth, watch the sunset with the kids, and spend a lot of time together. This is about the only thing in my life where I ever say that quantity is better than quality.

Even when you're busy, you have to realize and act on your priorities. One thing we all have in common is that we have 24 hours each day. To earn respect from the most important person, our child, we must figure out where we want to spend those hours and prioritize our kids. We all have work and other things competing for our time. Making sure that we find time for our kids as well as our other responsibilities is key.

We hear this time and time again: you need to spend time with your kids and be a positive influence. When I was working full time, I had to travel and be away from my family. But at the end of the day, I'd make sure to get a call in before my kids went to bed so that I could talk to them and still be part of their lives.

As divorced parents, you're still both raising your children, even if you aren't together. You're both helping each other be better parents. If you get divorced, you might not live with your child. That doesn't mean you shouldn't prioritize spending time with them. You still pick up the telephone and call. You still see them as much as possible. The adults in the relationship can monitor that, arranging times for the kids to be available. But if you're committed to being a parent worthy of respect, that's what you'll try to do.

The quantity of time is more important than the quality because quality might really mean that you're spending a little bit of time and rationalizing it as being enough. I once had an argument with a young, divorced man with a 5-year-old child, who was boasting about his quality time with his child. He mentioned how once, every month or two, he would take his child to the zoo, or the movies, or some other big event. I explained my position on how quantity with your child is so much more important to the child.

A child wants to be with his parents as much as possible, they love to wake up with parents and love to be tucked in by parents. I also suggested that the young man ask his child, "Would you like to see me every weekend just to hang around or once a month and go somewhere special?" He did that, and a few weeks later he thanked me for my advice. He learned that his child would rather have more time with him. To his child, the quantity of time was more important.

EARN YOUR CHILD'S RESPECT

As a parent, the challenge is to continually, beyond the shadow of a doubt, earn the respect of your children. That's a hard thing to do with so many negative influences bombarding kids all the time. That's why, as parents, we have to consider our own actions. A good test to determine whether there's something you should or shouldn't do would be to ask if you would want a clip about that decision to go viral? If you wouldn't mind seeing it online, do it—there's no need to say more. If you wouldn't want it going public, it's a good reminder to all of us to "rethink" that endeavor!

Relationships can become difficult as children grow older. The voyage from dependence to independence can be very tough on children and their parents. That's why it is a vitally important time to continue to strengthen those relationships. That's where the parents can strategize together and form a "unified agenda" in "how" they raise their children. What you want is two parents, but with one voice. When there are disagreements, it's hard to remember what is most important (the relationship). Most of the time, whatever we're arguing about doesn't really matter that much.

What is important is to sustain a good relationship with your children despite the issue at hand.

When I was young I had bell bottoms, I listened to rock and roll music, and I wore my hair long. My parents didn't like that at all. Similarly, today, I find myself wrestling with the tattoos and nose piercings that kids get; it's really difficult for me to agree with those decisions. What's important isn't the tattoos or the bell bottoms though, but how you manage the relationship. If a kid wants to get a tattoo, he thinks it's extremely important in the moment. But looking back, you'll find out that the tattoo was not all that important in the long run. Don't let a tattoo or any other disagreement keep you from continually growing the relationships that matter in your life.

It's easy to get caught up in temporary issues because they seem so important in the moment they happen. But as parents, always remember to focus on preserving the relationship no matter what the issue is at the moment. Working to keep strong relationships with your kids in all phases of their upbringing earns respect.

THE THREE SECRET KEYS TO STRONG RELATIONSHIPS

Relationships take work, and there will be arguments and disagreements, but we can learn from them. Be absolutely certain in relationships with your children, you verbally let them know you unconditionally love them:

1. Say it convincingly
2. Say it eye to eye
3. Say it more than once

Those three keys will help you create strong relationships with your children.

REFLECTION POINTS

FIRST – If there is a fight or a nasty disagreement, ask yourself a few questions.

- Could I have avoided this?
- Did I cause this?
- Did I miss something?
- How could I have handled this better?

When you dare to do that self-inspection, sometimes you'll find you're right and sometimes you'll find you're wrong. Sometimes you may need to alter the delivery of the message. But even if you're right and the other person's wrong, you can take the initiative to communicate with your child to better understand their position. Don't ignore it. And if you're wrong, admit it, and then apologize.

SECOND –Take the initiative to "right size" or rescue the relationship. If a sailboat is blown on its side, you want to get it back up and running right again. We call that "right sizing." You do everything you can to make it run again. In your relationship, it looks like you're trying to correct the conflict in order to strengthen it.

Whether you were wrong or right, don't give up on your relationship with your child, but try and right size it through communicating. Ask to talk about the issue some more and try to understand your child's position. Have the tough conversations that will lead to a right-sized relationship. That is what will lead to you being the kind of parent that deserves your child's respect.

THIRD – Refer to chapter one: forgiveness.

If your child is wrong, that's where forgiveness comes back into the picture. Keep trying and trying, but don't lose sight of the relationships that bring you TRUE happiness.

MAKE YOUR RELATIONSHIPS BETTER NOW

There are two things to focus on to make your relationships better now. First, as I've stated before, in terms of parenting the quantity of time is so important. You have to be there through the highs and low ebbs of your child's life to build consistent memories with them.

I know you're probably busy but think about it. Can you find time to take a shower? Can you find time to take your vitamins and have dinner? Those things aren't always convenient, but you find the time. And you have to do the same for your children. You find the time. You prioritize it. You cherish it. It's not a question of finding time; these are things you have to do and you *must do* in order to have TRUE happiness.

The second thing to focus on is respect. Treating others with respect is one of the major building blocks, the foundation of TRUE happiness.

If you're a respectful person, that's what you're going to get in return. If you're disrespectful, that's what you can expect in return. It's a very simple equation. Like we talked about in the beginning, we need to be worthy of our children's respect and we do that by being there and investing time in our families.

The original commandment is to "honor your father and mother;" we've talked throughout the chapter about being parents worthy of that honor and respect. When it comes to family relationships, treat your family in a way that makes you deserve respect. You do this by spending time with them and prioritizing those relationships.

The 4th Commitment to TRUE Happiness is: Invest time in all your family relationships.

"The children have been a wonderful gift to me, and I am thankful to have, once again, seen our world through their eyes. They restore my faith in the family's future."

—*Jackie Kennedy*

Chapter 5

NURTURE

"Thou Shalt Not Kill."

The fifth commandment is "Thou shall not kill." So what *should* we do instead of killing? I feel that the related commitment to happiness in this case means we should nurture and enhance the lives of others. We should build people's spirits up. We should not kill someone's future; we should enhance someone's future for the better. We should not kill the dreams of individuals; we should boost their dreams.

Nurturing others means trying to give them what they need to be whole and to feel alive again.

We should nurture all aspects of life, including our own well-being, as well as nurturing other people and their self worth, spirits, and endeavors. When we nurture, we help to improve, to make better, and to make more sustainable. Instead of gossiping and talking badly about people, we find the good in people and speak well of them. We nurture them when we uplift them with our words and look on the positive side.

Scientists from the National Research Council found many factors that contribute to a nurturing environment.

For children in the home, this means protecting them from harm, teaching and training them, and helping them understand the world.[13]

If we take these ideas and apply them to our lives, we can create a nurturing environment with all the people around us. We can try our best not to harm others, to share our insights with them, and help them feel seen and heard.

A study by UNICEF observed data from many different nations and cultures to see which children were the happiest. They found that those with higher quality relationships both in and out of their families were happier.[14] As we nurture others, we are helping to build supportive relationships that will increase their TRUE happiness and our own.

I was fortunate to be nurtured as a child by many of my family members. My older brothers nurtured my dreams of playing sports by teaching me how to play baseball, basketball, and football. My mother nurtured all ten of her children, in terms of spirituality, by bringing us to church and making sure we had a spiritual foundation. My hard-working father nurtured my work ethic by setting an example for me that I witnessed day in and day out.

I have worked to create a nurturing environment for people around me by using active listening, because that allows me to see where other people need help. For example, I was recently speaking to a man who was having a hard time at work with his boss. The more I listened, the more I was able to see that he needed to shift his perspective to

---

13   https://pmc.ncbi.nlm.nih.gov/articles/PMC3621015/

14   https://thelincolncenter.com/nurturing-childrens-happiness-the-im-pact-of-supportive-relationships/

make things better. Through some role play and powerful questions, he was able to realize some things he needed to change. The next time I saw him, I asked him how things were professionally, and he said, "Fantastic!" The active listening allowed me to help him come up with better solutions at work.

I try to nurture individuals on a personal level and on a larger scale as well with my charity work with Children's Flight of Hope (If you are interested in learning more, or getting further involved, please visit: www.childrensflightofhope.org)

NURTURING IN ACTION

The charity Children's Flight of Hope is heavily focused on nurturing families and making their lives better. Their mission is to fly critically ill children to specialized hospitals where they can receive needed treatment. Parents of these desperately ill children are willing to do whatever it takes to get help for their child, even utilizing all their finances, sometimes losing their jobs, to try to make their child well again. Giving families resources to help their children is a nurturing act because it gives them hope. We have heard from parents who have lost a child comment how they at least had hope for a long period of time, which they found invaluable. The one thing that I have noticed over the years is that all the volunteers with Children's Flight of Hope are very happy people. Nurturing others helps them achieve that great state of mind that I call TRUE happiness.

I recently met a young Army veteran named Anthony who has seen the effects of nurturing firsthand in an unusual way. He has a trained service dog that goes everywhere with him—even sleeps with him. He informed me that he contemplated suicide several times and that this dog has literally saved his life. He went on to say he has lost seventeen of his combat Brothers to PTSD-related suicide.

After seeing how this service animal nurtured his spirit and his emotional healing, this young Army veteran has made it his life's mission to raise money to buy dogs for other veterans suffering from PTSD to make their lives better as well. In this case, charitable giving is a form of nurturing that will in turn allow these trained dogs to nurture veterans. I was very influenced by him and promised to help him. We are currently forming a fishing tournament to raise money for this charity, and I feel certain that I will be supporting this charity for a lifetime.

The one major lesson that I have learned in fundraising for children and adults is that success is truly defined in terms of helping people in their time of need. Nurturing other people is a building block in the foundation of TRUE HAPPINESS!

NURTURING BRINGS HAPPINESS

When you nurture someone, you add to their happiness, and helping others to be happy brings happiness back to you. That's TRUE, lasting happiness. For example, when you give somebody a compliment, what do they do? They give you a compliment back. If you start nurturing others, it can be contagious. Additionally, if you give someone a compliment, how do you feel? You will feel good about yourself, knowing you made their day better.

Nurturing takes many forms. Nurturing can mean consoling, like when we nurture the widow who has recently lost her husband and work to help her through that season. Nurturing can mean being there when people are struggling and just rolling up your sleeves and getting involved. However you nurture others, it will help you to be happier, which I saw with my friend Bruce.

My friend Bruce Mortimer, who recently passed, took charge of a charity called Helping Up. Its mission is to help people in the Baltimore area who are facing homelessness, addiction, poverty, or other challenges.

Earlier in his life, Bruce struggled with alcohol addiction. He almost lost everything and truly hit rock bottom, but then he got sober and has stayed sober for 30 years. Because of his own challenges, he took a genuine interest in people and was someone who cared about the well-being of others. He has accomplished phenomenal things with his charity because of that desire. Helping Up has been able to serve over 18,000 individuals, and doing good for others in this way brought him purpose and happiness. The success of Helping Up is due to Bruce's desire to nurture those who faced some of the same challenges he had faced. It's a great example of what it means to nurture others to build a life that brings us lasting joy. Bruce was a happy man, always with a smile on his face. I certainly wish I had had the opportunity to get to know him earlier in life.

MAKE A COMMITMENT TO NURTURE

Nurturing doesn't have to be hard. It can start with a simple choice: to commit to sharing your time, talent, or treasure (resources) with others in need. Nurturing begins with a commitment to helping others which becomes a foundation for TRUE happiness. When you are around people helping other people, notice the expression on their faces. They're filled with smiles, even when their circumstances might be difficult.

It may feel at times like there are so many challenges and so many people willing to help, it may seem overwhelming to know where you can start to help. But don't give up. It won't always be easy to know where you can make a difference. There are going to be big challenges in the world that you can't fix on your own, but as you do your part to help and nurture, you won't fail as long as you don't give up.

Like we've talked about in other chapters, sincerity matters. When nurturing others, you do have to be genuine. You have to want nothing in return other than knowing how good you will feel inside. You have to truly want to help others. If you want to nurture somebody and help them with their problems, you have to expect nothing from them in return. What we're talking about here is changing your nature so that you can achieve TRUE happiness.

You can't fake it. If you are sincerely nurturing, this is going to actually change you. And that's why it matters.

In order to nurture others, you first need to notice that they need help. This means that when you see a need, you take action instead of ignoring it. If somebody needs to be nurtured, whether it's helping them increase their self-worth, their pocketbook, or whatever else they may need, work to become aware of it, and then take action.

THE SECRET KEY

The secret key to nurturing is to make your nurturing efforts ongoing. Think of it not like a handshake, where you quickly grasp hands and then let go, but instead like holding hands as you walk together.

This is because taking nurturing action is more than just a one time thing. When you commit to nurturing, commit with no time limit. Nurturing is not one good deed or a single action point. Nurturing is continued help that focuses on continuing the relationship. You'll know you have truly nurtured someone when you have become a part of their lives, and they treasure not just the help you give them, but the relationship that you have formed.

REFLECTION POINTS

Things to ponder in self-reflection

- How can I commit to nurturing others?
- How can I budget my time to help others?
- What challenges do I have with sharing my time, talent, and treasure with others in need?
- Who can I nurture right now?
- What can I do to make a difference in their lives?

You will have a great feeling about yourself, and about life in general, when you help other people, especially ones that can't help themselves—that is true nurturing and a step closer to TRUE happiness.

As the commandment states, "Thou Shalt Not Kill." Don't kill others' dreams, their hopes, their excitement.

Instead, nurture each of those and you will enhance their lives—and your own happiness.

The 5th Commitment to TRUE Happiness is: Nurture the lives of others.

"Competing at the highest level is not about winning. It's about preparation, courage, understanding, and nurturing your people and heart. Winning is the result."

—Joe Torre

Chapter 6

LOYALTY

"Thou Shalt Not Commit Adultery."

The sixth Commandment is "Thou shalt not commit adultery." Can you imagine learning about this commandment when you're young? I will never forget hearing about this when I was in grade school. Part of my education was learning from a book of questions and answers about the Christian faith. Each night for my homework, I had to memorize the answers to questions like "Who is God?" "Why was I created?" and more. I felt I knew the answers to most questions until I read the sixth commandment, *Thou shall not commit adultery.*

When I recited the sixth commandment to my mother, I asked her the question, "Mother, what is adultery?" If you can imagine a very conservative, strict, Irish mother who brought her children up without any type of sex education, you'll have a good idea of what her reaction was. I thought her eyeballs were going to pop out of her head! She stood up, waved her index finger in my face and said to me, "Joseph, that's none of your business." As young as I was, I was smart enough not to make another comment. I just nodded and said, "Yes Mother."

Like we have done with all the Ten Commandments, when talking about the sixth commandment, we want to focus on the positive: we know what not to do, but we need to know what to do for a happier life.

The sixth commandment is truly about loyalty, because when you commit adultery, you are being disloyal to your spouse. I believe this is one of the strongest commitments to TRUE happiness. Loyalty, defined as support, is rewarded time and time again by creating stronger relationships and a happier outlook on life.

Loyalty applies not only to marriage, but also to our families, our countries, our coworkers, our beliefs, and more.

Researchers who studied loyalty wanted to differentiate between loyalty that is tied to individuals vs. loyalty that is tied to more abstract things, like ideas. They discovered that greater happiness is found in *both types of* loyalty groups. In other words, when you are loyal to people *or* ideas, you will be happier. What's really interesting is that loyalty in one area (like which brand of toothpaste you buy, commonly called consumer or brand loyalty) is often correlated with loyalty in another area of life (like being a loyal friend).[15]

An honors thesis by Nathaniel Barry explored the idea that loyalty helps us feel like we belong to part of a group, which leads to greater overall well-being. This is true for political, social, and religious groups. Barry cites the work of Prilleltensky, which says that this belonging is likely due to the fact that, when we are loyal to a group, we feel like we

---

15 https://www.sciencedirect.com/science/article/abs/pii/
S0148296315002647

matter: we feel like we are valued and add value as well.[16]

I see so much loyalty in my life. I see it in friends, I see it in marriages, I see it in tight-knit families, I see it in patriotism for our country, and I see it between mentors and mentees—a commitment to helping another person. I am also loyal to my spirituality, and that creates a sense of belonging and happiness because it pushes me to do the right things. Like Nathaniel Barry said, my loyalty makes me feel like what I do matters, so I am more likely to do good.

LOYALTY IN ACTION

When you look at what loyalty really means, it implies having to choose what you will be loyal to. You can't be loyal to everyone and everything because loyalty often requires sacrifice. An example from the Revolutionary War shows us the level of sacrifice that may be required.

William Franklin, Benjamin Franklin's illegitimate son, was frustrated with British rule but didn't believe in revolution. Finding himself on the wrong side of leaders at the time (who were pushing for revolution), he was urged by his father and others to give up his views, but he refused.

Instead, William stood by his antirevolutionary beliefs, even when his home state of New Jersey chose revolution. He was sent to jail under terrible conditions, including solitary confinement. He wrote to a friend about his own suffering, saying that he would rather be "taken out and

16 https://www.sciencedirect.com/science/article/abs/pii/S0148296315002647

shot" than remain effectively "buried alive." Still, he didn't change his views.

When he was finally released from prison as part of a prison exchange, William continued to fight, becoming a loyalist leader and organizing attacks on patriot forces.[17]

This demonstrates two principles of loyalty. First, William knew what he believed, and he was loyal to it, not changing his views even when others were willing to. Second, he made sacrifices for his beliefs, choosing to be loyal instead of taking the easier path.

If we believe in something strongly, a natural consequence is our loyalty to that belief. One of the biggest challenges with loyalty is when something you are very loyal to, whether it be a political party, a sports team, or something else, makes changes that don't align with the reasons why you became loyal to them in the first place. You see this in politics today, whether you are a liberal or conservative, a Democrat or Republican; as the party itself changes, you may no longer have the same beliefs as the party.

That's why we need to understand what we are loyal to. Maybe it isn't a specific politician, but certain values that we feel deserve our loyalty. You have the right to change your political affiliation without that meaning you're disloyal. It means you're loyal to an ideal that once was accepted by your party. The ideal of that party changed, but your loyalty to the ideal remains the same.

Contrast that to family. I believe no matter what happens with your spouse, no matter how bad things get,

---

17 https://www.history.com/news/loyalists-revolutionary-war

it is valuable to stay as loyal as you possibly can until (and unless) the relationship reaches extremes you cannot move forward with.

Your spouse and your children deserve that loyalty. Sticking with them will bring you the TRUE happiness that comes from lasting relationships.

LOYALTY TO YOUR COUNTRY

Politics can cause the same damage and disunity as religion has (like in the Crusades, Ireland's Protestants vs. Catholics, etc.) Sometimes, here in America we hold our political affiliation to a higher regard than being a citizen of the United States of America.

So,to avoid the risk of causing offense to anyone, I will keep my personal political affiliation private. I have two friends, Tom and Ricky, who are on the opposite side of the aisle politically. As much as I disdain getting involved in political feuds, I also value having political discussions with those on the other side. Quite frankly, I am much more inclined to fight for Tom and Ricky than I am to fight against them, regardless of what party we support.

It is amazing how much the morals and patriotism of the three of us are aligned. Through respectful conversations, I have come to find out we have much more in common than I would have ever guessed. I believe the root cause of what makes these conversations successful is two-fold:

First – We all love and are loyal to our country.

Second – We have the utmost respect for each other as human beings.

LOYALTY IN MARRIAGE

At times, marriage can put our loyalty to the test. In marriage, we are fully committed to one person. But often, striving for our own happiness instead of our spouses can get in the way of making a marriage work. People get divorced because one person feels their spouse isn't making them happy. However—he or she isn't responsible for their spouse's happiness!

The truth is, I have a moral obligation to myself to be happy. You have a moral obligation to yourself to be happy. You don't marry someone to become happy. You don't have children to become happy. You are responsible for your own joy and happiness, just as everyone else is. It's not your responsibility to make someone else happy—BUT—at the same time, happiness *is* contagious.

And when you choose to be a loyal spouse, you will bring happiness to the marriage.

Sadly, there are times when tight-knit families face divorce, including my own. We all know the pain the children go through during a divorce, no matter how old they are at the time. This is where loyalty is vital. Parents should avoid arguing in front of the children and keep the divorce proceedings separate from them as much as possible. Instead, parents need a unified message to share with their kids about why they have chosen to go down the divorce path. More importantly, both parents must remain loyal to the family in spite of the divorce.

Loyalty to the injured family includes not competing for the children's love and creating a unified agenda during holidays. It is so important for each parent to reinforce the greatness of the other parent to the children. After all, children are created from these two people, so each parent can support the children in knowing that they came from someone great.

HOW LOYALTY LEADS TO HAPPINESS

TRUE happiness leaves clues. I always look at the happy people I know to see if these 10 commitments, including loyalty, apply to them.

From my observations, the happy people I've met all seem loyal to their religions, loyal to their political ideals, and loyal to their families. Disloyalty can be like a cancer that eats away at happiness, and loyalty is the cure. When you commit your loyalty to people, you will feel a sense of strength. Loyalty will strengthen the bond in your marriage, it can strengthen the bond in your family. Even when you have political ideals and beliefs that are similar to someone else's, the bonds of friendship can be strengthened.

When you're with other people who share the same ideals, you feel a sense of community. People who have similar likes, dreams, and hopes make you feel that you're not alone.

This feeling of connection is built upon loyalty. As you are loyal to ideals and loyal to people, you will feel more happiness.

CHANGING LOYALTIES

When the person or entity you are loyal to makes changes that are directly opposite of that which attracted you, you might say that individual or that entity was not loyal to their followers. In that example, it is very wise and prudent to make sure that you are loyal to what really matters to you. For example, if you vote for a politician who has your same beliefs about an issue, but that politician changes their position on that issue, it makes sense not to vote for that person anymore!

This decision isn't being disloyal. Like I said earlier, you have to have a deeper understanding of what you are loyal to. Are you loyal to certain beliefs and principles? Loyalty means giving constant support. Supporting what you believe in gives you integrity: what you believe must align with your actions.

THE SECRET KEY TO PUT LOYALTY INTO ACTION

"Who am I loyal to today?" is not something we wake up in the morning and ask ourselves. Yet it is critical to understand clearly who and what you are loyal to! That is when loyalty happens. You must be aware of your degree of loyalty as well, understanding the real issues and the people who are most deserving of your loyalty.

REFLECTION POINTS

- Where in your life do you see the need for loyalty?
- What is important for you to be loyal to?
- How can you increase your loyalty to the things and people that matter to you?

If you truly understand loyalty, you will also keep the sixth commandment, to "not commit adultery." Beyond that, you will also become more trustworthy. Loyalty will change the way you see yourself, since you will begin to see yourself as someone dependable and true.

The 6th Commitment to TRUE Happiness is: Let your loyalty be known and valued, as long as the loyalty is deserved.

"I have a loyalty that runs in my bloodstream; when I lock into someone or something, you can't get me away from it because I commit that thoroughly. That's in friendship, that's a deal, that's a commitment. Don't give me paper—I can get the same lawyer who drew it up to break it. But if you shake my hand, that's for life."

—Jerry Lewis

Chapter 7

GENEROSITY

"Thou Shalt Not Steal."

The seventh commandment is "Thou shalt not steal." This commandment is another example of being told what we're not to do, which leaves us looking for the more relevant commitment of what we are to do. What is the commitment? What should we do Inversely? As I pondered the idea of not stealing, I realized that the inverse of stealing is generosity.

If we want TRUE happiness, rather than steal, we need to share. We should be generous and share our time, talents, and treasures with people who need them or would appreciate them.

Studies show that if you want to be happy, the answer is to help others. Whether this is through donating money, spending time with others, or volunteering—generous giving increases our own happiness, health, and longevity. In a research study, high school sophomores were tested for biological markers that improve heart health and lower risk of heart disease, before and after a generosity intervention. After ten weeks spent volunteering after school, the students' health markers had improved, increasing the length (and the joy) of their lives.

In a survey of over 1,200 adults, the ones who gave most generously of their time and resources were also the most likely to say they felt God's love every day, a major contributor to happiness.[18]

Being generous with our time also has many benefits for us. Volunteering can help us feel like part of the community and create new friendships. A study done with older adults (age 55–94) showed that those who spend moderate time volunteering (up to seven hours per week) have higher life satisfaction overall.[19]

The generous people I know are all very happy people. The most generous person I know is a good friend named Ray. He was raised on a shoestring budget. Ray grew up, worked hard, and became successful, always remembering to help others along the way.

Back in 2024, Hurricane Helene decimated Western North Carolina. Ray hopped in his four-wheel-drive vehicle and traveled hundreds of miles to pay for and deliver generators to those who had lost power for in some cases days and weeks. Ray then drove to the destruction zones in North Carolina to donate the generators. The beautiful part of what Ray did is no one asked him to do it and he didn't tell a soul what he was doing. I only found out because I bumped into him in the mountains, and his truck

18 https://unlimitedloveinstitute.org/downloads/ITS-GOOD-TO-BE-GOOD-2014-Biennial-Scientific-Report-On-Health-Happiness-Longevity-And-Helping-Others.pdf

19 https://pubmed.ncbi.nlm.nih.gov/22391747/

was filled with mud. His generosity had a great impact on me—in inspiring me to be more generous with my time and resources like Ray.

In this chapter, we will focus on the concept of giving rather than taking. I saw the benefits of this in my own life when others were generous to me.

In 1980, I was asked to participate in a startup company. I was offered a very small weekly paycheck with a promise that if I did well and contributed to the growth of the organization, I would earn more shares in the company.

I am mechanically inclined and I have a pretty gregarious personality. These two traits earned me the job of fixing the company equipment and making it run, along with going out and selling something I knew nothing about!

Within a year, I impressed the two partners so much that they generously gave me one-third ownership stake of the company. This reward for my hard work was so generous. I was excited because I believed the company had a lot of promise for the future.

As time went on, the company grew and grew, and eventually, the new company was owned one-third by the employees and two-thirds by me. In 2020, the company was sold to a larger organization; this sale earned me a happy retirement. That would not have been possible without the generosity of the two partners in the early days of the company.

We all want to change the world for the better, but that wish is a difficult task to do. However, we can change the world for one person. It is amazing when I look back at the shares of the company I was given, which impacted my career and retirement. My world was changed because of another's generosity (albeit—generosity I worked hard to earn!). Their generosity might not have impacted the world, but it did impact my world.

TEACH YOUR CHILDREN GENEROSITY

It's critical that generosity be a pillar in any family. When my kids were young, I don't remember having a lot of conversations with them about being generous, but instead, I tried to teach them by example. Most often, they watched me participate in charitable giving.

Now that they are adults, I encourage them to be a part of my fundraisers, but the one rule I have is that they are not allowed to contribute to the same charity I support. Meaning, I want them to contribute to their own charities. I feel that if they give toward something meaningful to them, that will make it all the more impactful. At the same time, I like them to be at my fundraisers and see the generosity of others so it will inspire them.

When my kids attend the fundraising dinners for my charities, they can see people's smiles and the good time everyone is having. As people are generous, they get to experience TRUE happiness.

I saw a friend of mine teach this to his son. My friend is very generous and actively involved in charitable giving. His son wanted to follow his father's example of generosity. It just so happened that the son had an elaborate bourbon collection.

His parents suggested that he share with the less fortunate. The charity that his parents work with was giving to children, however, and he felt confused about how he could help. The kids obviously couldn't drink the bourbon!

His parents suggested that he donate the bourbon and let it be auctioned off and the proceeds given toward helping the children. Well, over a period of about five years, six figures have been raised for the charity because he was generous enough to put his collection of bourbon on the auction block.

Giving to people in need will allow you to experience more happiness than expensive bourbon ever could.

A few months ago, I was happy to hear that my own adult daughter and her friends put together a fundraiser for the flood victims in Western North Carolina. What was really rewarding for me is that she and her friends involved their children, who were all quite young. The kids started with lemonade stands, and local businesses donated items for the drinks so they were able to sell them at 100 percent profit. As a group, they were able to raise over $5,000 for flood victims.

My daughter felt so good that she said, "Dad, I want to do this every year." My daughter's and her friends' hard work and generosity set an example that their kids will never forget. These are things that schools cannot teach; these are things best learned by having parents set an active example.

WHEN GIVING FEELS HARD

Some people feel that they are not in a position to be generous, but I believe there isn't anyone in this world who has nothing to give. We all have 24 hours a day. We have our minds, our bodies, and if you want to be a part of something great, you can give what you have. Volunteering is a huge part of any charitable organization.

It's not giving money; but events and gatherings always need a team of volunteers. Without them, these things would not happen. So, think of being generous in three categories: time, talent, and treasure. We all have time. Many talents can open opportunities for us to give. For example, you might be able to play the guitar or be able to cook, and those are both talents that can help other people.

When you think of all the ways you can give, whether it be time, talent, or treasure, generosity can spread and grow.

I've seen this happen countless times. When you gather people in a generous circle, they join in and the generosity grows—and you become more generous yourself.

I saw that in action here on the island where I live. A family lost their home in a fire and people gathered to raise money to help. When we were all together, someone said, "This town needs a bigger fire truck."

We put together an event that involved people on the island. I suggested charging $25 a head to attend. A friend of mine said, "Are you crazy? People on this island have a lot of money. Charge $250 a head."

The goal was to have 100 people attend, and I thought that at that higher price there was no way we would fill the event. But between the charge for the dinner and the generosity of the people who attended, we were able to raise $400,000. We bought the town a new fire truck!

The point is, generosity spreads. It's contagious. When you see others give, you want to give too, because you can see that giving brings TRUE happiness when you observe it in other people.

GENEROSITY MAKES US ALL BETTER

As we're generous, we improve the world around us, and we also feel better. I see generous people all around me. There are many charities and foundations that benefit the needy around the world. When we involve ourselves and our families in being part of those charities, we share in the gift of giving.

It is helpful to remember that we cannot be generous to every organization and every person. I strongly suggest you pick your passions and make an effort to help there so you can have a bigger impact. TRUE happiness definitely stems from one's generosity. But TRUE happiness squared, TRUE happiness that impacts exponentially, comes from not only your generosity but from being part of an organization, serving on the board, or serving in a leadership role. This is when your TRUE happiness will certainly be magnified by the good you are able to do.

When I am raising funds for my own charity, I like to ask for money with the following phrase:

"Please don't give until it hurts; we're not here to make you hurt. We are here to help. We are actually here to make you feel good. Just keep giving until it feels good, until it feels really, really good right here in your heart."

And that's the point. Generosity feels good. Just try it and you will be able to see this in your own life.

THREE SECRET KEYS TO BECOMING MORE GENEROUS

There are three steps to acting with greater generosity.

First – be aware of all the ways it's possible to help. Pay attention to the TV commercials or observe the projects your friends are part of. If you go to church, you'll often see people put money into a basket. You'll notice that generosity is all around you if you take the time to notice.

Next – Figure out what you're passionate about. Is it children? Is it a specific country? Find your favorite need: it is more than likely there are organizations already helping to answer that need. You can volunteer your time and get involved.

Finally – Just get started! If you don't have money to give, give your time. If you don't have a lot of time, just give what you have.

"Remember that the happiest people are not those getting more, but those giving more."

—H. Jackson Brown

REFLECTION POINTS

- We all have the opportunity to give our time, talent, or treasure to others.
- Time: How much time could you donate to a good cause? When do you have time available? What are you willing to sacrifice to make time to be generous?
- Talent: What are your talents that you could use to help others? Maybe your talent is a labor of love, like

cooking a meal or taking someone with you to an activity.

- Treasure: What do you have to give? This could be money or something else. Ponder on what you have that you are able to give to others.

Beyond the seventh commandment to "not steal," we can also commit to being generous. Generosity with all we have brings happiness to our own lives and to others lives too.

The 7th Commitment to TRUE Happiness is: Be generous with your time, talents and/or treasures.

"All our relationships are person to person. They involve people seeing, hearing, touching, and speaking to each other. They involve sharing goods; and, they involve moral values like generosity and compassion."

—Brendan Meyers

Chapter 8

HONESTY

"Thou Shalt Not Bear False Witness Against Thy Neighbor."

The eighth commandment is "Thou shalt not bear false witness against thy neighbor." The inverse of bearing false witness, or telling lies, is to tell the truth. There are many dimensions of honesty and many ways it affects our lives and our happiness.

Honesty has a defined starting point: being honest with ourselves. Our own self-assessment of our honesty can start by accepting the fact that we are not perfect. When we acknowledge that we have weaknesses as well as strengths, we can let go of some of the needs we might feel to lie to make ourselves sound better than we are.

It is okay to feel uncomfortable about struggles and challenges. Knowing and accepting that we are vulnerable, and not hiding those weaknesses, is a position of strength that will allow us to be more honest with others.

Most of us value honesty, yet we struggle to be truly open and honest with others, which we can see in the research that has been done on this subject.

RESEARCH ON HONESTY

Studies show that honesty is one of the values people hold most dear. Still, most people lie at least a few times per day.

Sometimes we tell lies to spare others' feelings, but ultimately, even this type of lie can erode trust and harm the relationship. Honesty has the effect of strengthening relationships because it builds trust.[20]

Research that is especially relevant to the subject of happiness comes from a study done at Notre Dame. Over ten weeks, half of the participants were told to stop telling lies of any kind, while the other half had no restrictions on lying.

Each of the participants was tested weekly to monitor both their physical and mental health. Subjects took a lie detector test that was used to determine the number of lies they told that week. Interestingly, those who were focused on telling the truth had better markers of health. They reported less mental ailments (like being sad or stressed) and less physical ailments (like sore throats and headaches). They felt better physically, and their mood was better as well—they were happier!

This happiness spread to their personal relationships as well.[21] Telling the truth changes how we feel, making us happier, healthier, and more connected to those around us.

I have seen this in my own life. My company was competing for a two-year contract with a major

---

20 https://static1.squarespace.com/static/55917f64e4b0cd3b4705b-68c/t/59823ddbe45a7c447a3ac36e/1501707739848/lupoli.jampol.oveis.2017.pdf

21 https://www.apa.org/news/press/releases/2012/08/lying-less

pharmaceutical company. Though my company was rather small in comparison to the large publicly traded companies we were competing against, we won the contract, mainly due to the very competitive pricing we offered.

After about three months of doing business under the contract, my CFO informed me that we were losing money on this customer. I called a meeting with my managers to discuss this. It was brought to my attention that out of fear of losing the contract, we were too aggressive in reducing the bid price.

I made the difficult decision to be honest with the customer and tell him the truth, that we had given them a price we couldn't sustain. I expected the customer to have negative feelings and we risked immediately losing the contract. Instead, once he heard my explanation, he told me that he would get back to me the next day after speaking with his superiors.

The following day, I was asked to go back to the company and meet with the purchasing agent and his team. I expected an end to our business relationship because of our mistake. Much to my surprise, because we were honest and transparent, they were willing to let it go and continue our business relationship. We renegotiated a price with a small increase that brought us a little above the breakeven point.

Because I admitted to my mistake, greater trust was built, and the business relationship became more solid than ever.

HONESTY BUILDS TRUST

Zig Ziglar said, "Honesty and integrity are absolutely essential for success in life—all areas of life. The really good news is that anyone can develop both honesty and integrity."

Telling the truth can be hard, like in the example I just shared, but accepting the truth told to you can be hard too. If you're honest, that means you accept the truth even when it's painful. It can feel hard to tell the truth too, but when you're honest, there's a sense of relief—like weight lifting off your shoulders. Telling the truth gives you a freedom and peace of mind that you just don't have if you are telling lies.

I am fortunate to have friends who are very honest people. Our conversations are eye to eye, meaning we look each other in the eye because we don't have anything to hide, and that's why I have a lot of trust in these people. I also think they have trust in me.

Telling the truth builds trust, and trust leads to happiness.

The more honest you are, the more trustworthy you are. The more honest your friends are, the more trustworthy they are. When you are in relationships built on solid foundations of trust, you are less likely to second guess that connection because you know where people stand.

I was recently elected president of a private local dinner club. The previous leadership lost a lot of the members' trust because they kept things from them and were not as transparent as they could have been. Stepping into this position, my number one goal was to get trust back in this organization. So, I met with people face to face, I listened to what had happened and assured them that those were things of the past.

Trust in any relationship changes things. For example, if you trust a business you have a relationship with, you don't have to ask for fifteen quotes; you trust that you're going to get a fair price from an organization that has proven its integrity in the past. In friendship, you know you can rely on a friend when they say they're going to do something for you because they've been there for you consistently before. You'll trust that things are going to get done. That trust is built slowly, one honest interaction at a time.

HONESTY WITH OURSELVES STARTS WITH ACKNOWLEDGING OUR IMPERFECTIONS

To really be an honest person, you have to accept that no one is perfect. That means you don't have to hide, or be dishonest about, your own imperfections. I like to picture Pac-Man. It might seem like a strange example, but Pac-Man is a circle with a piece of pie missing, right?

I think that's what every human being is. We're not perfect. There's a piece of us that's missing, that will never be filled, because we'll never be perfect. None of us has ever met a perfect person.

But sometimes, our egos get in the way, and we can't admit that we are imperfect, and that leads to dishonesty as we try to cover that up. I think once we acknowledge that we're flawed and we make mistakes, then we can own up to our mistakes. The next step is to acknowledge that none of the people in our lives are perfect either, and that allows them to be honest with us about their weaknesses. Thankfully, we can get to the point where we can accept each other's shortcomings and let them be who they are.

We can be honest because we know that everyone is just that imperfect Pac-Man, and we're able to be easier on other people.

When we're honest about our own limitations and our own imperfections, we don't have to try to put on a front or pretend we're someone that we're not. This dedication to the truth will affect all areas of our lives, even little things like playing golf.

HONESTY IN GOLF

The following examples show how being honest in the small things matters, and both of them happened while golfing.

I met a bartender named Brendan many years ago at an Irish pub while he was working to become an American citizen. I developed a really good friendship with him. You could just see that he was a good person. One day, years later, he called me up.

He said, "Joe, I need a favor. I graduated from college, and I need a letter of recommendation. I'm applying to a big engineering firm and I'd really love to work there. Since you're the CEO of a company, if you could write a letter of recommendation for me, it would mean a lot."

As I thought about what to write and all of the good qualities this young man had, the thing that stood out to me was his honesty.

In my letter, I wrote that I played golf with Brendan once. On one fairway, he drove his ball into the woods, while mine went straight down the fairway.

I was on the green putting for par. I had about a 10-foot putt. And suddenly Brendan's ball appears on the green. I see the shot come out of nowhere. And he put that ball two feet from the pin. Then it was my turn to putt. My ball only went a couple of inches. Brandon said, "That's good for a bogey, Joe." And he made his shot, and I said, "Oh, nice par."

He said, "No. Joe, when I was in the woods, I moved the ball for my shot to get out, and that's against the rules. So, I got a bogey on this hole too." I wrote in that letter that it was the finest example of telling the truth that I'd ever seen. Brandon got the job. And every time we get together, he tells my kids about that letter and how it made a big difference in his life.

Golf is a game against yourself, and there are so many lessons about honesty in the game of golf.

Brendan's experience is a bit like that of Bobby Jones, a pro golfer in the 1920s. He was playing in the U.S. Open when he confessed to officials that he had moved the ball slightly and it needed to count as a stroke.

The officials argued with him about it, but he insisted that they add that stroke to his score. He ended up losing by that one stroke but by being honest, Bobby kept his integrity.

When we are truly committed to being honest, we tell the truth even when it would be easier or more beneficial in the short term to tell a lie.

LITTLE WHITE LIES

People often think of a white lie as any lie that doesn't really matter. They feel that white lies are about unimportant ideas or circumstances. Sometimes, we use the term "white lie" when we want to justify not telling the truth. The phrase "a little white lie," in my opinion, should only be used for good things, like a surprise for someone's birthday. A surprise party would benefit and celebrate someone you love, and soon they would see that your deception was intended to make sure they had a great birthday.

People might want to convince others that a lie was a white lie when really it was more serious than that.

An example of where we might not tell the whole truth is when the answer would be hurtful to someone else. Still, it's better to avoid the truth without lying, by somehow getting around the question when possible.

The truth can be very painful at times, and we shouldn't have license to tell what we perceive as the truth about someone else if we know that information will be hurtful to that person. The example that comes to mind is spreading gossip or things you have overheard. Sometimes, it's not your place to be truthful when it comes to sharing the hurtful opinions of others with the person they're forming those opinions about.

When it's a painful truth that you have the chance to share, sometimes the best course of action is to stay silent. You could answer a question that might be hurtful by saying, "I don't want to answer that because I'm not qualified to," or "I don't want to answer that because I might be incorrect." For example, I might not have all the facts and I might cause more harm than good if I share what I do know. In that case, I point the direction away from me to answer any related question without getting myself involved and I am still able to be honest.

Staying out of a complicated situation that doesn't really involve me gives me a better, cleaner feeling than getting involved and possibly causing more damage.

In difficult situations, we have to make a judgment call on whether to speak up or keep quiet. We can choose to avoid answering a question if the truth might be painful or destructive. But sometimes, we also see injustice that requires us to step in and tell the other person what happened. We each have to choose how to handle these different types of situations, and our responses should be aligned with the way we want to treat honesty and integrity.

TRUTH AND HAPPINESS

Is there a good time to lie? Unless there's a gun pointed at your head, and you could save somebody with a temporary lie, I can't really think of a good reason to lie. But the truth is, you also don't have to answer every question. Sometimes it's best to stay silent.

The only time you should be lying is in extreme cases, and the truth is, those things are not going to come up very often. So, whenever you can, choose honesty, because that will lead you to TRUE happiness.

THE SECRET KEY

The simplest way to be honest is by embracing more self-inspection and humility.

This includes being honest about how you feel. I think it's good to share your feelings with people and let them know where they stand, such as, "Hey, I consider you a good friend." "Hey, you're a buddy of mine." I try to verbalize such thoughts; I think it is a good way to practice honesty.

The same is true, if there's something that's bothering you. Get it out in the open in a respectful way. I think part of being honest is respecting each other's private issues if the other person doesn't want to talk. It can also mean having open conversations such as, "Look, I know you're struggling with this. I'd love to help you, but I don't know how. Can we talk about it?" That gives you an honest approach to something without barraging them with questions or saying the wrong thing.

I also want to add that to be honest with your opinion (what you think about something) is not the same thing as being honest with your feelings—openly sharing that part of yourself. When you feel like a relationship is safe, that deeper honesty of sharing how you really feel is the kind of honesty that deepens trust.

REFLECTION POINTS

- Reflect on what yesterday was like. Were you honest?
- Ask yourself: What am I going to do today? How could I live with more honesty and more trust?
- Now ask: How can I strengthen others by being more trustworthy?
- Reflect on the idea that you're not perfect. How can knowing this allow you to be more honest?

"Thou shalt not bear false witness against thy neighbor," says the eighth commandment. We have discussed choosing to be honest with ourselves and others. This commitment to a life of honesty makes us happier and strengthens our relationships.

The 8th Commitment to TRUE Happiness is: Be Honest With Yourself.

"Honesty is the first chapter in the book of wisdom."

—Thomas Jefferson

Chapter 9

RESPECT

"Thou Shalt Not Covet Thy Neighbor's Wife."

As you know this far into the book, like the Ten Commandments we have discussed, the ninth commandment focuses on what not to do. Rather than coveting your neighbor's wife, the reverse of coveting would be to respect, not just your neighbor's wife, but all the people you come in contact with. That includes respecting yourself.

When we respect someone, generally we admire them, usually because of their actions. Simply spending time with those we respect, whether it be our family, friends, or coworkers, increases our happiness. Even though the amount of time we spend with people and what we do during that time is highly individualized, the research shows that overall, these connections give us greater well-being.[22]

There is a strong link between respect and TRUE happiness. Do you know any really happy people that don't have and show respect for themselves and others? Respect is one of the primary ingredients you see in happy people. I think this is because if you are respectful to people and you

---

22 https://pmc.ncbi.nlm.nih.gov/articles/PMC7416486/

have self respect, you create positive energy which leads to confident, lasting relationships.

Additionally, studies show that the more respected you are, the greater your happiness is. In one such study, researchers studied MBA students through graduation and the start of their careers. Those doing the study knew from prior research that more money or great socioeconomic status does not equal more happiness. They theorized that when participants had more of a concept called "relationship status," which they defined as receiving respect from others you come in contact with, these graduates would often have greater happiness. They discovered that happiness varied based on how well respected these participants felt they were—not on money or social status.

Over the course of nine months, those in the study rated their happiness. Happiness levels continued to change depending on the level of respect they felt they received from others. This is interesting to note because when someone inherits a large sum of money for example, the effects on their happiness are very short-lived. Cameron Anderson, who authored the study, theorized that being respected by others and receiving their admiration "never gets old."[23] Whereas inheriting a large sum of money the benefits can feel brief when it's gone or spent.

As a father, I can say that the respect I feel from my children never gets old. When I spend time with my three daughters, I can't help but notice how different they are

---

23 https://www.sciencedaily.com/releases/2012/06/120620133310.htm#:~:-text=New%20research%20suggests%20that%20overall,stashed%20in%20your%20bank%20account

from one another, but one thing they have in common is that they each have a lot of self-respect and that they always treat me with respect. Being around people of mutual respect increases my happiness.

When the girls were young, we had a rule. I said, "As long as your last name is Elphick, you never boo anybody." I told them they could cheer for their own team as loudly as they wanted, but they couldn't boo. "Why Daddy?" they asked. I said, "Because we should welcome the opponents to the stadium and celebrate the game whether our team wins or loses." In essence, I was teaching my daughters to treat others with respect, even your opponents in life.

There are two kinds of respect I want to highlight here. One is the way you approach the world and treat others, even those you don't know. The other is a deeper respect that comes from knowing someone and admiring who they are. I learned this type of deep respect at a young age from my father. He treated others with respect and he commanded the respect of others by his integrity-based actions.

TREAT OTHERS WITH RESPECT

I come from a big Irish family of ten kids. As I mentioned earlier, we didn't have much money, but my father worked hard to provide for us, sometimes taking on two or even three jobs. As a kid, I knew how hard he worked and how much he sacrificed for our family.

One of the things he provided for us was an above ground swimming pool in the backyard that we would swim in all summer long. In the wintertime we would empty the pool to about 25 percent capacity, leaving a little water in the bottom that would freeze.

One winter day in New Jersey, I got in a little snowball fight with my friend. We were just fooling around. A snowball hit the liner of the pool and put a big rip in it. I said, "Oh my goodness, my dad's going to kill me." I didn't want to tell him. I didn't have the money to pay for it and I didn't know what to do.

But before I could do anything, he had a police report done and claimed it on his insurance. I had no idea this was going on. The pool got fixed and my dad didn't know what had happened.

In the meantime, I was saving my money, and a month or two later I handed him an envelope with the money to pay for the damage.

I said, "Dad, I didn't tell you at the time, but I'm the one that broke the pool. I was saving up and I wanted you to have the money before summertime." All these years later, I can still remember the smile on his face.

I respected my dad and the fact that he worked so hard to provide for our family and I did not want to let him down. I wanted to save up money as fast as I could to repay him because I respected how hard he worked, and what he did for our family.

CHALLENGES

Respect can show itself in many ways. I remember learning about the end of the Civil War in school, and one story that illustrates respect still stands out to me. It's been said that the Civil War was brother fighting against brother, but it was also former ally fighting against former ally. General Grant, under the Northern States, had to accept surrender from General Lee from the South. Grant and Lee had fought together against Mexico in the Mexican-American War. As victor, it was General Grant's right to seize property and weapons from Lee, as well as fire a 1,000 cannon salute. Out of respect for General Lee, General Grant refused. He chose instead to show respect to his wartime enemy.[24]

Respect seems to be a challenge in our society today. In fact, it seems that we are surrounded by disrespectful conversations, especially by people on social media. At times, people put things on social channels that are very negative for all the world to see. It doesn't have to be that way. Like I talked to my children about sports and not ever booing the opponent—the same thing applies online. Whomever you're talking to, or whatever you are talking about, find ways to cheer other people on rather than rip another person down.

What good comes out of disrespect? Nothing. More negativity creates more fighting. The more negative content you interact with, the more social media will send that kind of content your way, so over time it seems like the whole world is arguing and fighting with each other.

On the other hand, there's nothing better than social media when you respect somebody and you point out the good. This is especially meaningful if it's someone not related to you, like an old friend or classmate so that you can build them up. And seeing people make positive comments on

---

24 https://www.lifelords.com/story/respect-stories/

your content can really contribute to your TRUE happiness; you recognize the impact you had on others' lives. You can use social media to show them your respect and build others up rather than tear them down.

The same is true when we interact with people in person. I recently read a story about a man who was driving his family home one evening. He was going over the speed limit to try to get home so he could put his kids to bed. He saw the sight we all fear when we're speeding: flashing red and blue lights behind him. Pulling over, he rolled down his window to talk to the police officer.

When asked if he knew why he was pulled over, this man decided to react the way he wanted his kids to react: with respect. He admitted that he had been speeding and didn't make excuses. The police officer took his license and registration, but returned a few minutes later, saying that he had decided to give him a warning this time and that he appreciated that the man had treated him with respect.[25]

WHO DESERVES OUR RESPECT

It is my strong belief that each one of us can approach strangers with our "respect gauge" needles set to neutral. Meaning, respect is earned, so we probably won't respect someone we don't know. As we get to know that person, that needle will move a positive or negative direction in terms of respect.

However, whether we have respect for an individual or not, we can still choose to *treat* everyone with respect.

Sometimes we can be too quick to judge. For example,

25 https://www.lifelords.com/story/respect-stories/

I had a family member who met someone new and immediately said "I don't like that person. She's a snob." Two months later, they were best friends. This family member found out that the new woman she had met was just shy. That's why it's best if you start that respect needle on neutral. On that first day, my family member started the needle on the negative, disrespectful side. When we start relationships on neutral, we can avoid prejudging others.

However, a great challenge comes when you do get to know someone and you have determined that they aren't deserving of your respect. You've seen them in immoral or dishonest actions, for example. We can be tempted to treat them disrespectfully. But that's not the answer.

Instead, you need to remember the kind of respect we talked about earlier. Even if someone hasn't earned your respect, and you don't have a deep respect for them because of their actions, you can still choose to treat them with respect. That means that you would never say anything negative about them unless their actions were causing dangerous or problematic situations for someone else. Maybe you can't say anything positive either, so you choose not to talk about that person.

Respect is an ingredient of happiness. It's a commitment to TRUE happiness. So, choose to treat others with respect even when they don't earn it, and you will be happier because of it.

THE SECRET KEY

If you want to make respect a part of your life, the key is to verbalize it. Let others around you know how much you respect them. Let them know how much you respect others. Show them that you respect yourself.

If you respect somebody, why not let them know?

When you verbalize all these positive statements, it only creates positive energy. Those around you will feel happier because they are being respected, and you feel happier too.

REFLECTION POINTS

- Am I respected by others? Am I not respected by others? Why?
- Am I being respectful? Am I giving people the respect they deserve?
- Do I have and show respect for myself?

This chapter began with the commandment not to "covet thy neighbor's wife." Throughout the previous pages, we discussed the inverse: treating others with respect. Even when we don't feel respect, or others haven't earned our respect, we can choose to be respectful.

The 9th Commitment to TRUE Happiness is: Earn Respect by Being Respectful to Others and Yourself.

"Show respect to people who don't even deserve it; not as the reflection of their character but as a reflection of yours."

—*Dave Willis*

Chapter 10

APPRECIATION

"Thou Shalt Not Covet Thy Neighbor's Goods."

The final commandment, again, covers what not to do. For TRUE happiness, the reverse of being jealous of your neighbor is having appreciation for them and what they have. It can be easy for anyone to be jealous of those who have something you don't—take power or success as examples.

We see this when people start critiquing leaders in business or popular public figures in the media. Instead, you can appreciate that they have reached the pinnacle of their career and show them appreciation. We can celebrate with them by congratulating and supporting them. Appreciation comes in many ways, including saying or doing something nice.

When you're jealous of somebody, the opposite happens. You want to see them fail, so you might feel tempted to use your words to tear them down. When you appreciate someone, you build them up with kind words and actions.

There have been many studies done on happiness and what makes us happy. But scientists call appreciation a "mega-strategy" because it is literally one of THE strongest factors that determines our happiness.[26] Appreciation is strongly linked to gratitude, which we covered in Chapter 3. The main difference is that gratitude is internal; it's the feeling or, as the dictionary puts it, "the quality of" thankfulness. Appreciation is what we do with the feeling of being grateful when we express it to others or take the time to notice and enjoy all the good things in life. It would be difficult, if not impossible, to show true appreciation without first feeling gratitude.

When we feel gratitude and then share it with others, the results are fantastic. We will be more optimistic, better able to handle challenges, and more forgiving. We will feel better about ourselves and everyone around us.[27] It is worth diving into appreciation in this chapter, because the impact on our TRUE happiness cannot be overstated.

APPRECIATION HAS IMPACT

There is one moment in my career as a business owner where I received special appreciation that I will never forget.

We were meeting with a major pharmaceutical manufacturing customer to review a multiyear contract. My team met with their team for two to three hours to discuss our proposal. I was traveling and told my group I would be late to the meeting.

When I arrived, the meeting was almost over, and I simply asked how the meeting was going. I was told it was productive but that we had some conflicting issues with the contract. Before I arrived, the teams had agreed

---

26 https://www.rogerkallen.com/appreciating-a-key-to-happiness/

27 https://www.rogerkallen.com/appreciating-a-key-to-happiness/

to take the concerns home to discuss with each company's upper management. I asked if I could get a quick thumbnail description of the perceived conflicts.

I learned there were three main conflicts stopping us from getting this much-needed contract. Simply put, the three points were weighted positively to one side—their side. I addressed the group and suggested that we agree to all the parts they wanted added in the contract. My management team thought I'd completely lost my mind; the implications could be disastrous. The customer was very happy, until I mentioned that I would like each of these three points to also be mirrored on our part of the contract.

For example, the customer wanted to have an "out of contract clause," which meant the customer could cancel the contract for any reason with 30 days' notice. My proposal meant that we, too, could cancel for any reason with the same notice.

One of the managers on the customer's side stated, "That could shut our lines down and cost us a fortune." After a few minutes of silence, I stood up and stated this contract had to be a win-win. It wasn't here to destroy either company; it was there to help both companies become more successful. After a 30-minute discussion, everybody settled on all the terms in the contract. We agreed that a new contract with these provisions would be printed up and sent to us for signatures in the next few days. We all shook hands, and everybody left the table with the win-win.

After the meeting was over, the managing director of the pharmaceutical company pulled me off to the side and expressed his appreciation for what was accomplished in that meeting. He said to me: "Joe, we've never met before, but when you walked in the room, I felt like a great sense of leadership was now present." A lot of time has passed since then, but his sincere appreciation made a lasting impression and I will never forget it.

Appreciation builds confidence in the one who hears it expressed, and both the giver and receiver of appreciation are happier.

APPRECIATION IN THE WORKPLACE

Running a company gave me the opportunity to engage with a lot of my employees and I always tried to show them my appreciation. I feel that verbalizing and recognizing a job well done is more valuable than monetary recognition. Still, I would substantiate that verbal recognition with a pay raise whenever I could, because the employees deserved it for their part in helping grow the company.

When the manager told me that a particular employee was excelling at their job, I would not only give them a raise, I would also make a point to walk through the plant and thank that employee by name for all they did to build the company. I would pass on the kind things their boss said about their performance and express my own appreciation. When people feel appreciated, it grows their confidence in their own abilities.

At this point in the book, you might be wondering what my company did. We made paper boxes. One entry level position at my company involved using a high speed gluer/folder machine and literally reaching onto a machine, picking up a bunch of boxes, and putting them in a corrugated box for eight hours a day. It's a very necessary job, but it could be hard to keep people motivated. Recognition became an important part of keeping this job filled

I had one instance where an employee went the extra mile to show appreciation to all her coworkers. She asked if she could, at her own expense, make a birthday cake for every employee's birthday to recognize them on their special day. That small and simple act created a strong team who felt seen, noticed, and appreciated. Their self-worth increased; their productivity increased; and it became a happier work environment.

Feeling appreciated built a strong sense of community and positive energy throughout the plant. Being recognized for their efforts kept them motivated.

I noticed that showing appreciation to my employees encouraged them to do better and stay with us longer. Appreciation from my employees to each other—in this case, in the form of a birthday cake and celebration—helped them feel a part of something special.

Appreciation has widespread effects. Whenever we share our gratitude and express our appreciation, we uplift others and feel better in the process.

APPRECIATION ALL AROUND US

We live in a competitive society, and sometimes I see more competition than appreciation. In sports, there can be more booing than clapping at times. Clapping is a sign of appreciation that builds people up, while booing just tears the other team down.

When we're thinking about appreciation in the

professional world, I believe in capitalism, and that requires that businesses will compete with each other. But there's no reason a business owner can't also appreciate the good his competitors are doing, such as recognizing how many dollars another business spends on charities in the community. Competition doesn't mean we can't also show appreciation!

At the same time, in a family, we can show our appreciation verbally. Telling our family members what we appreciate can be spontaneous and quick. We can let them know we appreciate a meal that was made, or something that was cleaned up, or even the fact that they are choosing to spend time with us.

When we show appreciation to our children, this naturally opens up their hearts to us. We all want our kids to listen to us, right? Personally, I found that the only way I could get their brains to listen was first to get their hearts to listen. As parents, when we verbalize our appreciation, we set ourselves on that track.

We can also look for opportunities to show appreciation, even when it's hard.

For example, my daughter has a son who was applying for a private kindergarten at a very competitive school. There was a long waiting list and not every child would get in. But, we all thought my young grandson would be accepted. He's smart, he's funny, and he seemed like a perfect fit. So, my daughter was floored when they rejected him and wouldn't even put him on the waiting list.

My daughter and I talked about it, and when she asked for my advice, I told her not to worry about trying to convince them to let him in, but instead to accept their decision. "I know this hurt you, but" I suggested, "what you can do is be professional. You can ask them why and listen to the answer. Give them respect. And then maybe ask another question and thank them for every answer they gave you. Show them appreciation for considering your son as an applicant. Maybe with that information you'll be in a better position next year, and he'll get in."

My daughter did call the school and had the conversation. She said that it went extremely well. They were nice to her because she was nice to them. They explained the reasons her son didn't get in so she had some feedback for the following year. But even more importantly, they expressed appreciation for the conversation. Those school administrators admitted to my daughter that they hate making those calls to parents because the parents yell and scream at them. It was refreshing for them to have my daughter call and have an uplifting conversation instead.

When situations or relationships are challenging, it can be difficult to show and voice appreciation.

This reminds me of another story. I was raised Christian and when I was 12 years old, I would go to Confession. In my confession, I would say my sins out loud to the priest, and he would then give me my penance, usually something like "Pray five Hail Marys" or "Pray three Our Fathers." But on this particular day, the priest said to me, "Joseph, you are forgiven, but you have one thing to do: go to your enemy and do something nice for him."

I left that confessional thinking, "Now, how the heck am I supposed to do that?" But I had to do it as my penance. My "enemy" was a kid that I didn't like. In fact, I thought he was a real jerk. I went to him and gave him a compliment and a candy bar. He said, "Why are you doing this?" I said, "God told me to," and I walked away.

From that one small show of appreciation, the needle moved. I would never have given this kid a compliment of any sort because I didn't like him, but finding one small thing he did well, and expressing that to him changed our relationship. We got along better. I thought more highly of him and he thought more highly of me. If you think about it, appreciation has ties to many of the other commitments we have talked about: it can help us to forgive, to show respect, and to express our gratitude.

THE SECRET KEY

What is one thing you can do that will give you 80 percent of the results you want?

It's hard to compliment people you have a bad relationship with. Part of the reason is, in general, we haven't trained ourselves to look for things to appreciate in others and then say it out loud. And then, when we're experiencing stress, we find this that much harder. The key is to practice in nonstressful situations to practice thinking with appreciation and gratitude. So, to get some practice in, think about one person you could show more appreciation to.

My wife and I decided to try something new at the Chapel last week. We looked around to think about who we were grateful for there and then took the time to express that appreciation to them.

Later that day, my wife told me that it was a wonderful exercise to really reflect on all we are blessed to have in life and she realized how much we *don't* express our appreciation. I think we don't express it because we're not trained to do so. But when we make an effort to share appreciation with those around us we will realize it was worth the effort.

Sometimes appreciation does not come naturally. It's like your muscular system. If you don't exercise your muscles, they become weak. This component of TRUE Happiness demands exercise. You need to constantly think of how to appreciate the people in the world around you— and by all means express it as much as possible. Then, that appreciation muscle will becomes stronger. You will get more skilled at using it more often, and you will be able to express appreciation without much effort.

REFLECTION POINTS

- Let's exercise our appreciation muscles.
- When you wake up in the morning, take time to stretch your appreciation muscles and think of one statement of appreciation you would like to make to one person that day.
- Continue this as a daily exercise, and slowly start to add in more reps, working up to two or three appreciative gestures or compliments per day.

The final commandment, "Thou shalt not covet thy neighbor's goods," led to the topic of appreciation in this chapter. Appreciation is an expression of gratitude, turning our grateful feelings into action and words! Appreciation takes our happiness and spreads it around, multiplying the happiness we feel.

The 10th Commitment to TRUE Happiness is: Verbalize Appreciation Daily.

"Make it a habit to tell people thank you. To express your appreciation, sincerely and without the expectation of anything in return. Truly appreciate those around you, and you'll soon find many others around you. Truly appreciate life, and you'll find that you have more of it."

—Ralph Marston

SO, WHAT DOES ALL THIS MEAN...?

As the book winds to a close, let's take a second look at the question I was asked years ago at the debate I described in the introduction: Is religion good or bad for humanity?

Religion provides a moral fabric. It provides guidance. It's critical in a family and a society. But religion can divide us. Like politics can divide us.

In this book we have explored what can bring us all together. To do that we took the original Ten Commandments and reframed them into 10 Commitments to happiness that are not solely about religion or faith. Part of that reframing was to formulate them in a positive way of what to do to create TRUE happiness—instead of what not to do. They are about doing the things that will help bring out the best in each of us. They will bring TRUE happiness, the kind that lasts, even when the rest of the world is fighting and arguing over things that don't matter.

Let's revisit the commitments we've covered in this book.

The 1st Commitment to TRUE Happiness is: Choose to show your strength by forgiving others.

The first commitment is to **forgive**. It is truly a strong person who is able to forgive another person for wrongs that have been done. But when you exercise this strength to let go of your hurt, you don't have to carry that burden around any more.

The 2nd Commitment to TRUE Happiness is: Nurture human relationships with both kind words and kind actions and expect nothing in return.

Kindness is a commitment that will change who we are. We can look for opportunities to be kind every day, and to notice the kindnesses done by others.

The 3rd Commitment to TRUE Happiness is: Take quiet time to recognize what you have to be thankful for. The commitment to **gratitude** means that we cultivate an attitude of finding the good while also choosing to look at life in a positive light. Being grateful makes everything else that is going wrong in our lives seem just a little bit better.

The 4th Commitment to TRUE Happiness is: Invest time in all your family relationships.
Commit to your **family**! Spend quality time with them, and make your family relationships your priority. In 70 years of life, I can look back and say with certainty that those relationships mean the most to me and have played a huge part in my happiness.

The 5th Commitment to TRUE Happiness is: Nurture the lives of others.
Our happiness will increase when we take the time to nurture others. Nurturing means activity looking for ways to enhance the lives of other people, as well as finding ways to nurture your own well-being.

The 6th Commitment to TRUE Happiness is: Let your loyalty be known and valued, as long as the loyalty is deserved.

When you commit to **loyalty**, you become a more trustworthy person. Loyalty creates a sense of identity. When we are loyal, we know where we stand, and others know where we stand. It creates a sense of belonging.

The 7th Commitment to TRUE Happiness is: Be generous with your time, treasure, and/or talents.

Commit to being **generous**! If you want to be happy, share your time, talents, and treasures with others—and that happiness will come back to you.

The 8th Commitment to TRUE Happiness is: Be Honest With Yourself.

The commitment to being **honest** is one that will challenge us all. But when we choose to be honest—with ourselves and others—we are happier. We realize we have nothing to hide.

The 9th Commitment to TRUE Happiness is: Earn Respect by Being Respectful to Others.

Showing **respect** is a commitment that changes the way we interact with others. Remember, we may not feel respect for everyone, but we can always choose to treat others respectfully.

The 10th Commitment to TRUE Happiness is: Verbalize Appreciation Daily.

Finally, commit to **appreciation**. Appreciation takes what we feel inside (gratitude) and helps us share it with others to better their lives. I can't think of a better way to be happy!

None of us are going to live the commitments we've covered perfectly—I know I don't. We are all imperfect, yes, but we can all work to get better.

When each of us puts in effort to improve our own happiness, we can help all of mankind live in a better world. How? TRUE Happiness helps to improve our lives, and that happiness radiates outward to those around us.

I hope that after reading this book, you feel how close TRUE Happiness is. It can start to come into your life as you take one tiny action you've learned in these pages at a time. Maybe it starts with thinking about where you are now by going through the reflection points to exercise each commitment. Maybe it starts with doing one little thing differently in how you speak to or act toward others, or how you view the world. Those tiny changes will start to bring optimism into your life to let you know that TRUE Happiness is attainable.

People often say to me that I'm the happiest guy they've ever met. When I look back at my 70 years of life, it hasn't been easy. There were hard times, but I can see how these principles have made a difference for me.

When my first wife and I divorced, it felt like my whole world had ended and I would never be happy again. It took time to heal, but what helped me more than anything was to look forward each day, choosing the things that would build happy moments in my life again.

I learned then that I am the one in charge of how I feel and I made a commitment to my own happiness.

My wish for you is that through reading and using this book, you truly become happier.

And when you are happy, you will want to share that with others. So, if this book has helped increase your own happiness, share it with someone you care about.

I also would love to hear from you. I have thought of 10 Commitments to happiness, but I know there are other commitments that you are probably living right now that help to make you happy. Will you share those so we can all increase our happiness by sending me an email at truefulfillment@fastmail.com?

When my daughter went to college, I told her that I had one expectation for her as she completed that experience: that she would make the world a better place.

As my wife and I went to visit her, we met her roommate's parents and they said, the only thing we want for our daughter is for her to stay out of jail. My daughter turned to me and said, "See, Dad, all they want is for their daughter to stay out of jail, and you want me to make the world a better place!"

So I'm asking you to do the same thing I asked my daughter. I believe it is possible for each of us to improve the world, one person at a time.

Improving the world is really about making a difference in people's lives one by one. Start with you. Use these commitments to become happier. Then, share that happiness with others around you, and you will have made this world a better place, one person at a time.

To your happiness,

Joe Elphick

truefulfillment@fastmail.com

AFTERWORD

They often say to "give until it feels good," but Joe Elphick takes it one step further—he gives until others feel good along with him. His generosity is not just an individual act; it is a force that inspires, uplifts, and brings people together in support of something greater than themselves. His commitment to Children's Flight of Hope (CFOH) is more than financial; it is deeply personal, rooted in a belief that every child deserves access to life-changing medical care, no matter the distance.

Joe has given his whole heart to our mission and the children we serve, standing by us through some of the most challenging times. When the road ahead seemed uncertain, he was there—ensuring CFOH could keep the lights on, keep hope alive, and keep children and families on their journeys to healing. His unwavering support was not just a bridge over hardship but a foundation for growth, allowing CFOH to emerge stronger, more resilient, and more capable than ever.

Today, CFOH stands as a thriving and growing organization, serving more children and families than ever before. And behind that strength is the generosity of a man who saw the need, stepped in, and made a difference that will be felt for generations to come. Joe's legacy is not just in what he gave but in the lives he changed—and in the countless others he continues to inspire to do the same.

Pat Nelli

President & CEO
Children's Flight of Hope

Please visit www.childrensflightofhope.org

ABOUT THE AUTHOR

Joe Elphick's greatest pride and joy are his three daughters, and the title he holds dearest is "Dad." His newest and most rewarding venture? Becoming "Papa."

A lifelong entrepreneur, Joe built a business from the ground up, starting with little more than determination and a vision. Over four decades, he grew his manufacturing company into a thriving enterprise, producing folding cartons, medical leaflets, labels, and more for the pharmaceutical industry. After selling the company, he stepped into a well-earned retirement.

These days, Joe stays busy serving on boards, consulting, fundraising, cooking, golfing, and offshore fishing. His love for North Carolina's coast and mountains is reflected in his homes on Bald Head Island and Linville Ridge.

Through it all, Joe has found that true happiness is fueled by "classy people" around him:

CLASSY PEOPLE DEFINITION:

"People who continually help others—even those they do not know—and ask for absolutely nothing in return."